DR JONATHAN TOOG

The story of the Somerset surgeon
who founded Bridgwater Infirmary

by

Lesley Sutcliffe

Self-published 2017

ISBN 978-1-5272-0826-1

Printed by Remous Print, Wyvern Buildings,
Milborne Port, Sherborne DT9 5EP

For my husband David
and our children Amy and Thomas
and for my parents,
who gave me the opportunity to study medicine

"A single doctor, like a sculler plies
The patient lingers, and he surely dies;
But two physicians, like a pair of oars,
Waft him with swiftness to the Stygian shores."

Poem accredited to Dr Henry Sully
and frequently quoted by Dr Jonathan Toogood

CONTENTS

Giles Family

John Giles = Mary Saunders
1754-1804   1759-1852

Joseph	William = Sophia	Susannah	**Ann = Jonathan Toogood**	Nancy	Robert	Joseph	Maria
b/d 1782	1783-1853	1785-1787	1786-1875	b.1787	1789-1829	1793-1886	1794-1880

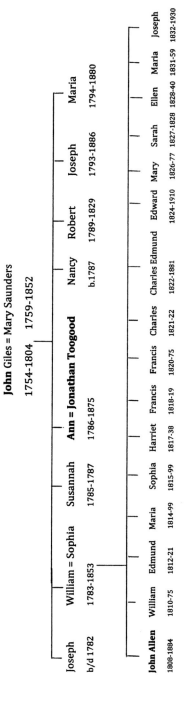

John Allen	William	Edmund	Maria	Sophia	Harriet	Francis	Francis	Charles	Charles Edmund	Edward	Mary	Sarah	Ellen	Maria	Joseph
1808-1884	1810-75	1812-21	1814-99	1815-99	1817-38	1818-19	1820-75	1821-22	1822-1881	1824-1910	1826-77	1827-1828	1828-40	1831-59	1832-1930

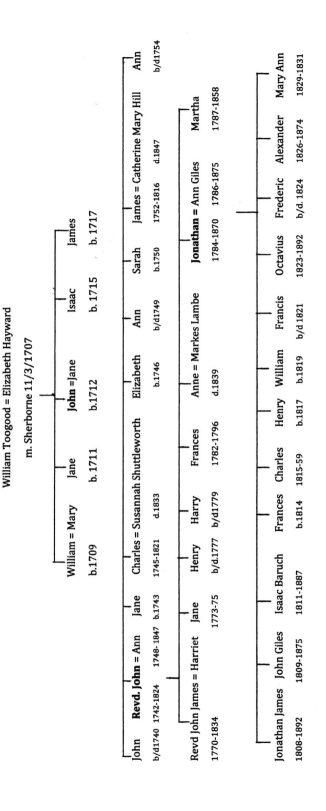

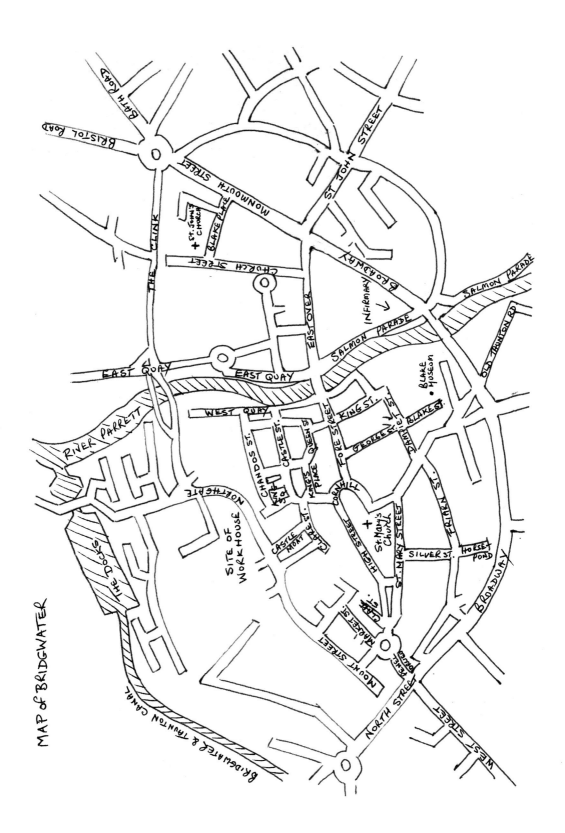

MAP OF BRIDGWATER

Preface

Dr Jonathan Toogood was born at the end of the 18th century and entered the medical profession at a time when it was still imbued with ancient theories passed down through the centuries from Hippocrates and Galen. Taught by eminent medical men of their day, he went on to witness many of the changes that transformed the practice of medicine in the 19th century – most notably the emergence of anaesthesia.

He was from a deeply religious family, whose members strove to improve the lives of their fellow men. He worked hard throughout his life, keeping an open mind and embracing new ideas in order to improve the care of the sick. His main claim to fame in the west country is the founding of Bridgwater Infirmary in 1813, although this achievement has long been forgotten and his name is no longer remembered by today's inhabitants of this once prosperous port in Somerset. In addition he held strong views about other current issues that concerned the medical profession at that time – specifically homeopathy, coroners' courts and arsenic poisoning.

In the Somerset Heritage Centre there is a book entitled 'Somerset Worthies', written by Robert Kinglake, which lists in alphabetical order the names of people who were considered worthy of this title. Under the 'Ts' in the corner of a page, someone has written in pencil – 'J Toogood, Bridgwater surgeon.' I hope my book goes some way to rectify the fact that his name was not included in this list and at the same time to give the reader a glimpse into the life of a surgeon in 19th century England.

Lesley Sutcliffe
Isle Abbotts,
Somerset April 2017

Chapter 1

A Sherborne Family

'. . . men who are not content with being thought good-enough,
but aspire to the vain-glorious title of TOOGOOD'
Revd J. Peddle, curate of Sherborne, 1777

This snide 'put down' was directed at John Toogood, a worthy gentleman of Sherborne, whose grandson Jonathan is the subject of this book and who himself was targeted by the same punning criticism nearly 50 years later.

Jonathan Toogood was born in Kington Magna near Sherborne, Dorset in 1784, the fourth of five surviving children and the second son of the Revd John Toogood and his wife Ann. Three older siblings (Jane, Henry and Harry) all died as infants in the 1770s. Jonathan's older brother John James (b1770) went to Trinity College Oxford and became curate of Gillingham (Dorset) and then Rector of Writhlington (North Somerset). He moved away to Wiltshire in 1802. Jonathan's sister Frances sadly died in 1796, aged only 14. Another sister Anne married Markes Lambe, a surgeon from Yeovil and she is buried at Sherborne Abbey (d1839). His youngest sister Martha (b1787) remained a spinster and chose to look after her parents in their old age, dying herself in 1858.

Jonathan was 14 years younger than his brother and chose not to follow him to Oxford but embarked instead on a career in the medical profession. That decision took him to the town of Bridgwater in Somerset in 1798, where he would make a huge contribution to community life over many years and fulfilled the promise of his aspirational Dorset family.

The Toogoods were a well-known and respected family in Sherborne. There are records of the family dating back to the 17th century. Jonathan's great-grandfather William Toogood, who died in 1732, was described as a rich draper in the town and lived as a tenant at Sherborne House, a large Palladian house, which had been extended from its Tudor origins in 1720. Its walls and ceilings were painted by Sir James Thornhill, a famous decorative painter of that period who had been commissioned by Henry Portman, the owner of the house at the time.

Plate 1: Sherborne House
Author's photo

John Toogood (b1712), Jonathan's grandfather, was the third child of William Toogood and Elizabeth Hayward, who had 4 other children – William, Jane, Isaac and James. John was educated at King's School, which later became known as Sherborne School. He became a Governor there in 1746 at the age of 34 and spent the next 43 years working tirelessly to maintain high standards of teaching and discipline within the establishment. He was Chairman of the Governors in 1752, 1764 and 1776 and was not afraid to criticise the conduct of the headmasters during his years at the school, sometimes harshly, describing one as a 'frozen snake'. From his writings he comes across as a deeply religious man, who had a strong work ethic and despised those who were only interested in their own career advancement. It would appear that John Toogood could be very difficult to please and was probably a thorn in the side of a number of individuals, but his heart was in the right place and he probably didn't deserve the comment made by Revd Peddle at the beginning of this chapter.

Tucked away in the archives of the Dorset History Centre in Dorchester is a leather-bound notebook, belonging to John Toogood and written in beautiful, bold script entitled *A Gift of an Affectionate Parent to his Children*. It appears to have been written in his later years and gives the reader a first hand account of events that occurred in Sherborne in the 18th century. John Toogood was known as an 'opulent mercer' – by that time Sherborne had become a prosperous town, due mainly to the wool and linen industries. Later in the century silk throwing became more important and in 1753 a silk throwster by the name of John Sharrer from Whitechapel in London leased Westbury Mill, converting it for silk production. In his book John Toogood tells of his own involvement with the town and the school and there are also snippets of advice for his children.

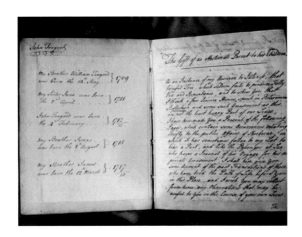

Fig.1 Notebook of Jonathan's grandfather John Toogood
courtesy of Dorset History Centre

In his notebook, John has nothing but praise for William, Lord Digby who died in 1752, describing him as 'full of Days, good deeds and just honour, whose benefactions contributed to the support of public worship of God in this Place, and whose benevolence often fed the Hungry and clothed the naked inhabitants of this town'. He was not quite so enamoured by his successor and grandson Edward Digby, remarking to his children: 'Here you see, as you so often will, the love of money superior to the cause of religion'.

John tells of his membership of the Sherborne and Shaftesbury Turnpike Trust, serving alongside his brother William from 1753 until 1756, when they resigned in objection to the number of tollgates being constructed, concerned that it would affect trade. He describes the corn riots in the town in 1757. These were in part provoked by his own brother William, a local farmer who sold his wheat at a high price that year, and this caused a great deal of upset throughout the town. John stepped in (with others) to ensure that poor families had a sufficient weekly allowance of wheat to make bread at an affordable price and peace was eventually achieved. In response to a letter in the *Sherborne Mercury* condemning the farmers, he wrote a letter in their support but it was never published. However, his advice to his sons if they found themselves in farming was 'let not a covetous eye tempt you to be foremost in advancing the price of corn, but rather let your behaviour shew compassion and charity towards the condition of the poor, who do sensibly feel the Distress of such times'.

In 1748 John was an Overseer of the Poor and was therefore responsible for distributing funds to the needy, known as 'outdoor relief' – a system dating back to Queen Elizabeth I's reign. This would change in the next century with the Poor Law Amendment Act of 1834, which resulted in the workhouse system. Like so many towns at this time the Sherborne streets would have been dirty, the houses had no running water and there were only outside privies. Infections were common – in 1740 and again in 1748 there were serious outbreaks of smallpox in the town. John was also one of the Brethren of the Sherborne Almshouses and, as with his dealings with the school, he was not always impressed by his fellow board members, complaining that they were 'inattentive to the more essential parts of the trust' with 'seldom any proper measures taken either to prevent the wrong or execute the right'. The Almshouse of SS. John in Sherborne was founded in 1437 and was purpose-built; the building is still being used today as a home for the elderly.

Plate 2 Sherborne Almshouses *author's photo*

Jonathan Toogood would have been aged 11 at the time of his grandfather John's death in 1795. He would certainly have known him and may well have been influenced by his work ethic and attitudes. Many of these characteristics are recognizable in Jonathan – he was not afraid to voice an opinion, ruffle a few feathers, set high standards and devote his whole life to the medical profession, which he held in such high esteem.

τ

Turning to the next generation of the Toogood family, Jonathan's father (another John) was born in Sherborne in 1742, the eldest of seven surviving children (three others died in infancy). John attended King's School, like his father before him, and went up to Oriel College Oxford in 1760. John was awarded a BA in 1763 and a MA in 1766, and after ordination was given a living at All Saints, Kington Magna in 1768 by his father, who was a benefactor of the church. Kington Magna in Dorset lies in the Blackmore Vale between Sherborne and Shaftesbury, the surrounding countryside featuring in Thomas Hardy's novels. All Saints Church is Norman and was described as a 'small and antique structure' at the time when the Revd John Toogood took over the living there. It was later extended in the middle of the 19th century.

Plate 3
All Saints
Kington Magna
author's photo

In contrast, the Old Rectory is a substantial Georgian house situated at the other end of the village. It was here that Jonathan Toogood was born and spent his childhood. After 56 years of service, Revd Toogood died there in 1824 and Jonathan's mother moved away to the nearby hamlet of West Stour, where she was looked after by her daughter Martha until she passed away in 1847 at the great age of 99.

Jonathan's father Revd Toogood was a man of deep convictions and wrote theological discourses on the 'wisdom and goodness of God'. He also addressed letters to the 'Gentlemen, Clergy and Freeholders of Dorset' on the subject of the African Slave Trade. Three of these letters, plus one addressed specifically to the clergy of the county of Dorset, were published in Sherborne and are still in print today – the original publications are held at the British Library. Unfortunately they are not dated, although one was written on 26th December, reminding the inhabitants of Dorset that it was the season of goodwill towards men. The letters were probably written sometime between 1784 and 1789, as he starts one letter with the opening sentence 'The alarm of war having subsided'. This probably refers to The Paris Peace Treaty of September 1783. Elsewhere he urges the readers 'to direct your Representations in Parliament to introduce a bill for the abolition of that dreadful Pre-eminence in wickedness, the Traffic of human Liberty.' William Wilberforce would make his famous speech in May 1789. Thomas Clarkson, arguably one of the most influential British campaigners at the time, formed, with eleven other committed men, the Committee for the Abolition of the African Slave Trade in 1787 and from then until 1794 wrote pamphlets and books available to the wider public.

The letters written by Revd Toogood are very moving to read, as he describes the capture of the slaves from their own lands 'hunted, like wild Beasts'; the dreadful conditions and treatment of the men on the slave-ships; and the selling of them to 'the best bidder' when they were 'branded on the breast with hot iron'. He relates an account given to him by a West Indian planter from Antigua, who described, in a matter of fact way, the horrific punishment handed out to those who tried to escape. He writes: 'My Blood ran cold, and my Heart died within me.' Two other letters are very much in the same vein, again pleading to the people of Dorset to speak out against the slave trade: 'To exert ourselves in this great cause, Gentlemen, is not merely an act of charity and mercy, it is what reason, equity, and justice demand'. The letter, addressed to the 'Clergy of the County of Dorset,' refers to Thomas Clarkson's report indicating that the slaves were not given Sunday as a day of rest and prayer.

An appendix at the back of the published letters describes a meeting that took place in Dorchester in 1792 of a number of the Clergy of the County of Dorset. They had met to consider a petition to Parliament for the 'Abolition of the Slave Trade'. A clergyman, who is referred to as the Revd Mr. E gave a 'long harangue' against the measure. Revd Toogood takes each of his points and argues eloquently against them. The petition was agreed to by one hundred and eleven of the clergy, Mr E the only one opposing it!

The abolition campaign remained dormant after 1794, perhaps due to Clarkson having a breakdown, no doubt as a result of spending several years on the campaign trail up and down the country. However, in 1803 the campaign started up again. Wilberforce tried once more to push the Abolition Bill through parliament but it failed in 1804 and 1805. It wasn't until February 1807 that the Bill to outlaw the Slave Trade, meaning the trafficking of slaves, was passed. Slavery, the actual ownership of slaves, in the British colonies was not abolished until 1833. Thomas Clarkson wrote a comprehensive history of the fight to get an Abolition Bill passed including details of his many travels, entitled *History of the Rise, Progress and Accomplishment of the Abolition of the African Slave Trade* and in this he mentions that he had received a letter from Revd John Toogood in support of the cause.

As a young man, no doubt Jonathan heard about his father's principled stand against slavery, but was also impressed by another clerical member of the family – his uncle Charles (his father's younger brother). Charles was rector of Broadway near Ilminster in south Somerset for some years. Of a keen evangelical and dissenting disposition, Charles was remembered by friends as a witty, refined and generous man.

It is clear that the young Jonathan received from all these family members a formidable example of a liberal, progressive and principled life, dedicated to the betterment of his community and society. They were powerful role models!

Chapter 2

Starting Out

In order to keep pace with the improvement of the times, he [a medical man]
must preserve a teachable state of mind, still consider himself a student,
and not despise information, from whatever quarter it may come, more
especially if it be the result of observation – always remembering that the
old see afar, that they stand on the height of experience, as a warder on the
crown of a tower   Jonathan Toogood

Jonathan Toogood was just 14 years old when he left Kington Magna to
start a medical training as an apprentice surgeon-apothecary in the town
of Bridgwater, Somerset in 1798. This was with Messrs Dawe and Anstice
and is listed in the UK Register of duties paid for Apprentices' Indentures
(*Fig.2*). Mr Hill Dawe, an established surgeon-apothecary in the town, had
been training apprentices since 1763, while Mr William Anstice, an
apothecary from Wellington, had moved to Bridgwater and taken on
apprentices since 1785. Both were clearly experienced trainers.

Fig.2 from Apprentices' Indentures (1710-1811)

Why Jonathan chose Bridgwater remains a mystery but it proved to be a
good start for him and in time very beneficial for the town. There may have
been family connections but one possible link may be that in 1785
Bridgwater was the first town to send a petition to the House of Commons
supporting the abolition of the Slave Trade. Thomas Clarkson visited the
town soon afterwards and met with a number of influential people,
including a Mr (Robert) Anstice, ship-owner and merchant, who was the
brother of Mr William Anstice the surgeon. Could it be that Jonathan's
father also met with the Anstices to discuss the abolition campaign and
remained in contact with them?

In later life Jonathan wrote a book of his memories of his medical career
and this will be referred to in greater detail in later chapters. Suffice it to

say that from this book one can pick up snippets of information about his years as an apprentice to Mr Dawe. He speaks of him warmly as 'my old friend' and describes how his 'old master' had gained a considerable reputation for his treatment 'of dropsy and diseases resulting from slow inflammatory action'. His five years as an apprentice allowed him to see many cases right across the spectrum of illness and gave him the tools to undertake the treatment of the sick.

τ

The medical profession at that time looked quite different from what it does today. Medical education is now fairly standardised with medical students attending a university affiliated to a teaching hospital, but until the second half of the 19th century it was somewhat haphazard. It was not until the first Medical Act in 1858 that a medical register of all approved practitioners was established. Practitioners were then required to have specified entry qualifications to be listed in the register and they alone were eligible for public employment – in other words there was a tightening up of the system.

At the start of the 18th century, the medical profession had long been divided into Physicians, Barber-Surgeons, Apothecaries and Itinerants – the latter frequently referred to as Quacks. Physicians underwent their training at one of the universities, namely Oxford, Cambridge or Edinburgh. It was a long training (anything up to 12 years) and involved little or no practical instruction. They studied philosophy, anatomy (by textbook) and botany, the latter being important as many medicines were derived from plants. The study of 'physic', referring to disease and treatments, was still based on the teachings of Hippocrates and Galen. They did not undertake any treatments that involved soiling their hands; that was left to the Barber-Surgeons, who would do the blood-letting and bone-setting along with other 'surgical procedures' such as removing bladder stones, treating cataracts and pulling teeth! Physicians were the diagnosticians and in old paintings are generally depicted as being well-dressed (suggesting a certain status), gazing up at a flask of urine; whereas the Barber-Surgeons are usually shown drawing blood from a patient in not such salubrious surroundings. Physicians were the only members of the profession who were permitted to use the title of 'Dr' and earned the letters MD after their name. On the other hand, surgeons were referred to as 'Mr', and even today doctors revert to this title (or the female equivalent) after they have completed their surgical training – a vestige from the past.

In 1745 the surgeons split from the barbers and slowly their status began to rise, so that by the end of the 18th century their place in society had improved but it was still below that of the Church and the legal profession. There were far more surgeons and apothecaries than physicians. For example, the 1783 Medical Register (more a trade directory) lists one physician but seven surgeons and apothecaries in Sherborne. It was common practise to combine the roles of surgeon and apothecary and this was really the forerunner of today's General

Practitioner. Eventually surgeons became more hospital-based as soon as voluntary hospitals started to appear, while some apothecaries chose the retail route and became known as druggists.

Unlike physicians, the surgeons and apothecaries learned their trade as apprentices, very much a practical form of training. The parents or guardian of any apprentice would pay a lump sum, or premium, which would cover training, board and lodging for up to seven years. An apprenticeship was secured in several ways – through family connections, by recommendation or by advertisement. The premium could be very expensive depending on the status and reputation of the master, but the average was about £60 in the provinces at the end of the 18th century (about £7,000 in today's money). It wasn't until the Apothecaries' Act in 1815 that all apothecaries were required to attend lectures in anatomy, botany, chemistry, materia medica (pharmacology) and the theory and practice of 'physic', as well as spending six months working in a hospital. They were then entitled to obtain a licence to practise from the Society of Apothecaries.

At the end of the apprenticeship the young man (of course it was always a man) could become an assistant to a practitioner with the hope of setting up in practice on his own or, if more able, he could seek to become a pupil of a hospital surgeon to complete his surgical training. Some found it difficult to get work and there was considerable competition for patients; others turned to parish work and were given annual contracts, while many used midwifery as a way to build up their practice and increase their income.

Before the 18th century, women had been totally responsible for the care of women in childbirth but the 1700s had seen the advent of the 'man-midwife' and the increased use of instrumentation at delivery, with forceps and other more brutal instruments. Many practitioners jumped on the bandwagon and the female 'midwives' were pushed off the scene. These surgeons did not necessarily have any special training, only what they had learned during their apprenticeship and there were cases of unnecessary meddling. The Apothecaries' Act had not included a midwifery qualification as one of the requirements to obtain a licence, and it was not until the Medical Act of 1886 that midwifery qualifications were listed in the Medical Register. It took another century for midwifery to be recognised as a respectable female profession.

There were a number of practitioners who did not prosper in the profession and others who resented the long hours that accompanied the work, often trekking through the night on bad roads to outlying villages to attend the sick. Some managed to change their profession and others inherited money or estates and spent the rest of their lives as comfortable yeomen. It must be remembered that medicine was closed to the female sex; this would only start to change in the second half of the 19th century when some very single-minded women took on the male medical establishment.

At the end of his practical training in 1803, Jonathan left Bridgwater to further his surgical training as a pupil of Mr John Abernethy, a surgeon at

9

St Bartholomew's Hospital in London and founder of its medical school. At that time students decided their own curriculum, choosing which lectures to attend. Jonathan must have been an able student to have obtained such a position and probably needed to have financial support from his family. For example, a year's residence and tuition at St Thomas' and Guy's Hospitals (known as the United Borough Hospitals) cost about £150 in 1801 (about £18,000 in today's money).

Plate 5 John Abernethy
(1764-1831)
Wellcome Library

St Bartholomew's Hospital and Priory were founded in 1123 by the monk Rahere and were intended for the sick poor in Smithfield in the City of London. Rahere had started life as a court jester but decided to reform his ways, after experiencing a vision of St Bartholomew while on a pilgrimage to Rome. The Priory was eventually closed in 1539 at the time of the dissolution of the monasteries but Henry VIII granted the hospital to the city in 1546. Many famous names are associated with the hospital – one such is William Harvey, who is best known for discovering that the blood circulated around the body. He was appointed physician in 1609. The hospital escaped the Great Fire in 1666 but was rebuilt in the 18th century and continues to prosper on the same site today.

Before continuing with Jonathan's own story, we should look more closely at that of his mentor John Abernethy, as Jonathan would get to know him well over the next two years. By 1804 John Abernethy was a well respected teacher and much liked by his pupils. Dr George Macilwain, another pupil of Abernethy, wrote a moving account of this man entitled *Memoirs of John Abernethy*, first published around 1830. It sheds a great deal of light on the work and character of a man, who today seems to be only remembered for his abrupt manner. John Abernethy was born in

London in 1764, the son of a merchant. He was sent away to Wolverhampton School, where he was noted to be a quick and passionate boy – very humorous but a good scholar. His only failing was that he was hasty and impetuous, all characteristics that remained with him during his entire adult life. He was apprenticed in 1779 at the age of fifteen to Sir Charles Blicke, surgeon at St Bartholomew's Hospital. Abernethy didn't care for this man, who had a very lucrative practice and appeared to be only motivated by financial gain – something that was of no interest to Abernethy then, nor at any point in his life.

At that time there were no anatomy lectures taking place at St Bartholomew's, so, as well as attending lectures given by Percivall Pott and John Hunter (both famous and influential anatomists and surgeons of the 18th century), Abernethy attended lectures (*fig.3 left*) at the London Hospital (now the Royal London), given by Sir William Blizard whom he much admired and liked.

William Blizard was born in 1743. Following his apprenticeship, he completed his studies at the London Hospital in Whitechapel in the East End. This hospital had been founded in 1740 and by the end of the 19th century was the largest voluntary hospital in Britain – even in 1800 it had 450 beds.

LECTURES at the LONDON-HOSPITAL, 179?.

ANATOMY and PHYSIOLOGY,
Mr. *Blizard* and Mr. *Orange*,
Monday, the 1st of October, at One.
** *Private Instruction, in the anatomical Room, from Ten till One.*

The THEORY and PRACTICE of PHYSIC,
Dr. *Cooke*,
Friday, the 12th, at Eleven.

CHEMISTRY,
Dr. *Hamilton*,
Saturday, the 13th, at Ten.

MATERIA MEDICA,
Dr. *Hamilton*,
Monday, the 15th, at Ten.

MIDWIFERY,
Dr. *Dennison*,
Saturday, the 13th, at Eleven.

CHIRURGICAL PATHOLOGY and PRACTICE,
Mr. *Blizard*,
Saturday, the 20th, at Seven in the Evening.

CLINICAL CASES,
Drs. *Cooke* and *Hamilton*,
Monday, the 22d, at Twelve.

** *Mr.* VAUGHAN, *Apothecary, at the Hospital, will acquaint Students with Particulars.*

Fig.3 Lecture List
London Hospital

Plate 6 *right*
Sir William Blizard
(1743-1835)
Wellcome Library

11

Blizard spent the whole of his career as a surgeon at The London and lectured in anatomy, physiology and surgery. It was William Blizard who introduced 'walking the wards', meaning that he would teach his students on the wards at the patient's bedside but always stressed the need for dignity. In 1785, together with the physician Robert Maclaurin, he persuaded the hospital to allow the building of lecture rooms and thereby the Medical School was founded. John Abernethy went on to say of him: 'My warmest thanks are due to him for the interest he excited in my mind toward those studies and for the excellent advice he gave me to direct me in the attainment of knowledge.' When Abernethy retired from the College of Surgeons, Sir William, by then an old man but still working, observed of Abernethy 'that his life has been devoted to the improvement of the healing art'.

Jonathan Toogood was fortunate to acquire from Abernethy not only the same professional desire to improve his skills but also an open-minded approach to medical knowledge more widely. For Abernethy had by now become an eminent scientist as well as a surgeon, interested in chemistry, conducting various experiments and writing papers on the skin, lungs and digestive tract. He only conducted experiments on himself and on dead animals, for he abhorred cruelty and did not approve of vivisection. He became passionate about lecturing, teaching both anatomy and surgery, even on his wedding day! There is no doubt that his pupils loved him and enjoyed his style of teaching. His lectures were full of anecdotes and humour but he was never vulgar and used simple language. Benjamin Brodie, a contemporary of Jonathan's, wrote in his autobiography:

> 'Mr. Abernethy was an admirable teacher. He kept up our attention so that it never flagged; and that which he told us could not be forgotten. He did not tell us so much as other lecturers, but what he did he told well. His lectures were full of original thought, of luminous and almost poetical illustrations, the tedious details of descriptive anatomy being occasionally relieved by appropriate and amusing anecdote...Like most of his pupils, I learned to look upon him as a being of a superior order.'

Sir Benjamin Collins Brodie, as he became known, is famous for his work on the diseases of bones and joints, and was surgeon to the Royal Family.

Abernethy's lectures attracted more and more students and in 1790 the Governors at St Bartholomew's agreed to build a new lecture theatre (opened in 1791), leading to the eventual foundation of the medical school by 1822. In 1796 Abernethy became a Fellow of the Royal Society and in 1814 was appointed Professor of Anatomy and Surgery to the College of Surgeons. He was eventually appointed chief surgeon to St Bartholomew's in 1815, by which time he was beginning to suffer ill health but he remained there until 1827 when he resigned.

On the personal side, he had a happy marriage and enjoyed being with his large family. As to his character and manner, it is true that he could be brusque and rude to his private patients, especially initially, but they soon learned of his compassionate nature. He was never unkind to his hospital patients and was always happy to visit the poor, often not accepting a fee. On occasion he would delay a visit to a Duke in order to visit an impoverished patient who he felt needed his services more urgently. He would say 'never perform an operation on another person, which, under similar circumstances, you would not have performed on yourself.' He cared nothing for money and declined a knighthood, the latter of no importance to him. He died in 1831 having suffered for many years with 'rheumatism' and associated valvular disease of the heart.

He contributed a great deal to the study of physiology and surgery, and was remembered fondly by his pupils. Jonathan Toogood was one of those, describing him as his 'estimable preceptor, to whose kindness and instruction I am mainly indebted for my success in life', a comment rather reminiscent of Abernethy's view of Sir William Blizard. He also recognised in him that character, which can be best described in his own words: 'his kindness was as great as his manner was uncourteous'.

As a pupil of John Abernethy, Jonathan would probably have lodged with him in his home at Number 14 Bedford Row.

Plate 7 Abernethy's house at 14 Bedford Row *author's photo*

Today this is a wide, elegant street of Georgian houses near to Gray's Inn in the borough of Holborn but back then, although the houses were relatively new, the street would have been bustling with horses and carriages. Underfoot there would have been mud and filth, and water would have been drawn from a water pump (which has since been preserved). A walk from Bedford Row to St Bartholomew's may have seemed quite challenging to a young man brought up in the Dorset countryside. He would have had to walk through Holborn (well known for its slums) and the streets could be dangerous due to high levels of crime, especially at night. We know, for example, that Sir William Blizard carried a weapon with him for self defence in the form of a broad sword, which became known as 'Blizard's hanger'!

Jonathan would have been expected to undertake dissection of the human body as part of his instruction in anatomy. At this time corpses were scarce, as legally only the bodies of murderers who went to the gallows could be used for dissection – the origin of this goes back to the time of Henry VIII. During the course of the 18th century, with a rise in the population and an increase in the number of medical students, there were not enough bodies to go round. This led to the unscrupulous and illicit trade of supplying corpses to the Anatomy Schools and the perpetrators became known as 'body-snatchers' or resurrectionists. Graveyards were in poor condition and overcrowded at this time and so it was easy to lie in wait and exhume a fresh corpse. Provided the 'body-snatchers' removed only the body and left the shroud and other accompaniments, no real law had been broken – the human corpse itself didn't constitute property. It became quite a lucrative business for some, as surgeons such as John Hunter and Sir Astley Cooper paid as much as £10 for a corpse. There were also various scams, involving undertakers – for example, bodies were switched in order to provide a younger corpse.

Many schemes were employed to try and thwart the resurrectionists. Families would stand guard over the grave for several days until the body would no longer be suitable for dissection; various types of metal coffins were produced; some graves were encased in iron railings (known as a Mortsafe); and there were many other inventions devised to protect the graves. Some graveyards had a locked dead house where a body could be kept for a few days before burial.

Although the idea of dissection was very distasteful to most people and also to many surgeons, there was the underlying acceptance that the study of anatomy was essential for medical students and surgeons. There was, however, the dilemma that Christians believed in physical resurrection and if the body had been stolen, this could not happen. By the 1820s the debate was beginning to hot up and in 1828 Henry Warburton MP suggested that the House of Commons appoint a Select Committee to inquire into the subject of dissection. Forty men were called to give evidence, twenty-five from the medical profession – one of those was John Abernethy – while the remainder were public servants, such as London magistrates and police officers. Surprisingly, there were also three resurrectionists. The Bill put forward was to deter the 'unlawful disinternment' of bodies and at the same time to regulate the schools of Anatomy. It became legal to use the unclaimed bodies of those dying in workhouses, hospitals, asylums, prisons and those found in the street – in other words the poor. The initial bill failed but it was eventually passed in late 1831. This time the scandal around Burke and Hare in Edinburgh and the 'London Burkers' (Bishop and Williams) had become known. Instead of stealing the bodies, they had turned to murder in order to obtain corpses for the anatomy schools. These events acted as a catalyst to getting the Bill passed and it became known as The Anatomy Act of 1832. It was not repealed until 1984 and the fear of dissection associated with workhouses remained until well into the twentieth century. Bodies are now bequeathed for dissection to medical schools and there were further changes in 2004 with The Human Tissue Act.

τ

Jonathan obtained his membership of the College of Surgeons (MRCS) in May 1804 and worked on the wards as a 'dresser' at St Bartholomew's. This would have involved tasks such as admitting the patients onto the wards, assisting in the operations, laying out the surgical instruments and dressing wounds. During this time he would be gaining the experience he would need for his future career. He returned to Bridgwater in the year 1806 to start life as a Somerset surgeon.

Source: Anonymous. *Rahere Ward*, 1823 in Whitteridge G, Stokes V. *A Brief History of the Hospital of Saint Bartholomew*, 1961.

Fig.4 Rahere Ward, St Bartholomew's 1823

Chapter 3

Return to Bridgwater

I will use my power to help the sick to the best of my ability and judgment; I will abstain from harming or wronging any man by it - part of the Hippocratic Oath

Jonathan Toogood returned to Bridgwater in 1806 and set about establishing his practice. The town's population by now was approaching 5,000. It is unclear where he first found lodgings but by 1822 the Pigot's Directory lists him as living in the Cornhill, and he was still shown residing there in the 1841 census. He must have had a horse for transport in order to visit his patients in the surrounding villages, his son Jonathan James refers to borrowing his father's phaeton (carriage) in the 1830s. Jonathan himself describes visiting a farmer's wife out on Sedgemoor who had pneumonia, commenting that the area was 'an aguish locality, in which hundreds of acres were often flooded for months'. Ague (acute fever) – or what we recognise today as malaria – was still around at this time in England, especially in marshy districts where the mosquitoes could breed. The parasite was most likely *Plasmodium vivax*, which has a lower mortality than *Plasmodium falciparum*, the most dangerous type. The medical profession was still unaware of the association of this disease with these insects and thought the fever due to 'bad air' or miasma (the word malaria comes from the Italian *mala aria* which means 'bad air'). Superstition was also a prominent feature of country life. Even in the 1830s his eldest son, who was later to become vicar at North Petherton (a nearby town), tells of a young woman who was suffering with the ague and had paid 6d to a farmer for a religious charm that she was told to wear 'in her bosom'. It consisted of the following writing from scripture:–

> *When Christ saw the place where he should be crucified, all his bones did shake. Jesus said. I have neither ague, agony nor fever and whosoever have these words about them shall never be troubled with ague, agony and fever. So Lord Jesus keep all sick persons in six days, if it be thy blessed will, in the name of the Father, of the Son and Holy Ghost.*

On 24th November 1806 Jonathan, aged 22, married Ann Giles, aged 20, daughter of the recently deceased Mr John Giles of Southwick House in Mark, a village about 10 miles north-east of Bridgwater.

Plate 8 Southwick House, Mark *author's photo*

How they met is unclear but it is quite likely to have been during the time he was apprenticed in the town. Ann's father John Giles, born at High Hall in Mark, had inherited Southwick House and the accompanying estate from his first wife Ann Starr. His second wife was Mary Saunders and Ann was the fourth of their eight children. Like his father William before him, John Giles had served as church warden to the Church of the Holy Cross in Mark, in which there is a plaque dedicated to him and his wife Mary.

Plate 9 *left* Plaque to
John Giles,
Church of the Holy Cross,
Mark village
author's photo

Plate 10 Church of the
Holy Cross, Mark village
author's photo

It was here that Jonathan and Ann were married. They certainly didn't have a very long honeymoon, as Jonathan writes that on 5th December (12 days after their wedding day) he was called out to see a strong thirty year-old man, who had dislocated his knee joint after falling off a wagon laden with coal! During Jonathan's forty years as a Bridgwater doctor, Ann had to adjust to his long working hours and his many meetings that took him away from home. Jonathan was one of five surgeons in Bridgwater and he not only took on patients in the town but also undertook parish relief work outside the town in the village of Bawdrip (3 miles away) at a modest annual salary of 7 guineas. He and Ann lived in the centre of Bridgwater – the Cornhill was the old marketplace, surrounded by shops and the nearby bustle of the port. Together they had 12 children – 10 sons and two daughters *(see Chapter 13 for fuller details)*. The oldest child Jonathan James was baptised by his grandfather Rev John Toogood back at Kington Magna but subsequent children were baptised at St Mary's Bridgwater, Revd William Wollen conducting seven of these ceremonies. Dr Wollen, vicar from 1785 until 1844, lived in Castle Street and was known to be a rather stern man and the last vicar to have worn a wig!

As regards family life and schooling, the oldest child Jonathan James (b1808, always known as James) went initially to Bridgwater Grammar School, originally founded in the mid-16th century but beginning to lose its reputation and its pupils by 1819. At age 10, he transferred to Dorchester Grammar School, where he was joined by his cousin John Allen Giles. James then went to Exeter Grammar School and on to Harrow. It is likely that the other children were educated at Dr Morgan's School in Bridgwater, which was established under Dr John Morgan's will of 1723. By the 1820s it had a new schoolroom seating 300 boys and was providing a good grounding in elementary subjects. It did not, however, become a secondary school until 1871. It later moved, was renamed Haygrove Comprehensive School in 1973 and continues today. It is not known where the other boys went to secondary school but three went on to become surgeons; two trained as solicitors and two joined the Indian Army. In the 1841 census the Toogood household is recorded as having three female servants, so Ann probably had considerable help raising her large family over the years. In addition, Ann's widowed mother Mary was on hand for a few years at least, having moved to nearby Friarn Street, while still caring for Ann's younger brother Joseph (b1793) and sister Maria (b1794).

τ

The Toogood & Giles families were, therefore, quite close during this time, the latter producing some rather interesting and notable characters in the course of the century. Jonathan's brother-in-law William Giles was educated at Bridgwater Grammar School and his parents hoped he would enter the church. However, he appears to have preferred the life of a farmer, taking over the family farm at Southwick House in 1804. Jonathan's children visited their cousins on the farm on a regular basis. In 1817, however, William Giles moved to Frome where he had invested a great deal of money in a carrying business. But the investment proved to be disastrous and William, who knew nothing about the business, lost £10,000 over the course of the next 20 years. In the 1841 census his occupation is described as a 'carrier' and this was a common form of employment in the 18th and 19th centuries. Carriers would transport people and goods from place to place and were important prior to the coming of the railway. At one time he found himself in the law courts in Taunton and was committed to Wilton Gaol (Taunton) for what reason is unclear, but we do know that the gaol at that time was used for those guilty of felonies, misdemeanours or breaches of the peace rather than for debtors.

William Giles married Sophie Allen and together they raised 16 children – six born at Southwick House and the others in Frome. Despite William's rather colourful early life and financial problems, his eldest son John Allen

Giles (b1808) was educated at Charterhouse School and went up to Corpus Christi College Oxford, becoming a Fellow there in 1832. His mother Sophie then persuaded him to enter the church and accept a living at Cossington, a village 5 miles north of Bridgwater. He was, however, reluctant to give up his interest in the legal profession and was certainly not suited for the life as a country clergyman. In 1838 he obtained his DCL (Doctor of Civil Law) and was also a scholar of Anglo-Saxon history. In the 1830s he was appointed Headmaster of Camberwell College School and then the City of London School but failed to be successful in these roles and in the 1840s became bankrupt. He upset the Bishop of Oxford by challenging Church Doctrine and in 1854 he was jailed for the illegal Solemnisation of Marriage. In 1867 he took a living in Sutton, Surrey where he remained for the remainder of his life. He had married Anna Dickinson in Bridgwater in 1833 and theirs was a long and happy marriage. Their eldest son Herbert became Professor of Chinese at Cambridge University and one of Herbert's sons, Dr Lionel Giles, became Keeper of the Oriental Printed Books and Manuscripts at the British Museum.

William's other sons prospered – William junior (b1810) became a solicitor in Taunton; Francis (b1820) was a medical practitioner in Stourbridge in Worcestershire; and Charles Edmund Giles (b1822) became an ecclesiastical architect and lived in The Crescent, Taunton. He was the founding secretary of the Somerset Archaeological Natural History Society. Jonathan and Ann must have stayed with him on occasions, as there remains some correspondence from Jonathan quite clearly written at The Crescent.

Returning to Ann's siblings, Joseph Giles, nine years younger than her, became a Captain of the 9th Regiment of Foot in 1813 and was about to join Wellington in Belgium in 1815 when the news arrived that the war had ended with the Battle of Waterloo. After retirement from the army, he became manager of Stuckey's Bank in Wells, and in 1861 he was treasurer of The Union, Parish and Board of Health Officers in Wells.

Ann's mother Mary Giles left Bridgwater and went to live in Frome with her son William and in the 1851 census she is shown as being 91. Ann herself also lived to a good age and appears to have remained in good health, for we see her visiting her family across the country these family connections are further explored in chapter 13.

τ

Bridgwater was a very different place back then. In 1801 the population was 3,634 and consisted of working men and women linked to the busy port. The town is cut in two by the River Parrett, a tidal river that flows into the Bristol Channel. The first stone bridge connecting the east and west sides of the town, was built in c.1200 and later replaced by an iron bridge, cast at Coalbrookdale and completed in 1748; it was the only bridge until later in the 19th century. Ships could navigate the river right up to the bridge and consequently the town became an important port. It imported coal from South Wales, wool from Ireland as well as wine, iron, salt and herrings, along with other produce from neighbouring ports. Bridgwater also traded with places as far away as Newfoundland, Portugal and the West Indies. It exported unfinished cloth, known as 'Bridgwater' and agricultural products such as peas and beans. By the 18th century ship-building was a very important part of the town's economy along with the brick and tile industry, which continued into the next century. 'Bath Bricks', made from the clay collected from the banks of the Parrett, were used for scouring purposes, and were exported along with the building bricks and tiles.

The population in the 19th century increased dramatically – by 1841 it was 10,430 and although parts of the town were prospering, the poorer inhabitants were experiencing overcrowding and were living in poor housing surrounded by insanitary conditions. Sewers emptied directly into the river Parrett and water was taken from Durleigh Brook, at one time passing through a series of wooden pipes to the town's cisterns and water pumps, one of which was under the High Cross in the Cornhill. The latter was demolished around 1800, leaving the town dependent on wells, rainwater butts and the Durleigh Brook, all water being carried by hand to the houses. Water from wells became contaminated by seepage from shared outdoor privies and closets, which were often sited next to water pumps. It is no wonder that diseases such as dysentery were a common problem. The Durleigh Brook, which empties into the River Parrett, was eventually dammed in 1938 to form the Durleigh Reservoir.

There was no street lighting until the gas works was established in 1834. The roads were cobbled and described as 'abominable and in places impassable', while the back alleys leading into the courts were filthy. Refuse and human waste were collected by the night-soil men and sold to farmers for manure. There was certainly a great deal of poverty and most work that was available was low paid.

A study of the 1841 census gives a clear picture of the occupations in the town. There were the usual tradesmen – butchers, bakers, grocers, ironmongers, fishmongers – even a tripe seller, as well as laundresses, collar-starchers and chandlers. There were the semi-skilled often plying their work at home such as shoe makers (cordwainers), bonnet makers, seamstresses, tailors, stay-makers, clock makers, carpenters, stone-masons. Around the docks were housed mariners, shipwrights, sail makers and merchants. Brick makers and tile makers were numerous, as were agricultural labourers. There were the inevitable publicans – Bridgwater had a total of 63 inns and public houses at this time, and of course there was a need for ostlers, saddlers and blacksmiths. Alongside these folk were only a handful of what we would describe today as professional people rubbing along together side by side in the same streets. Jonathan's immediate neighbours in the Cornhill were a tailor and grocer. This was to be the community that Jonathan would spend the next thirty years administering to in his practice, and in time in the Infirmary.

The Cornhill at the beginning of the 19th century still had the old timber framed market house and the High Cross with the cistern holding the town's water supply. In the 1820s the market house was demolished and replaced by a new, rather more elegant, colonnaded building, while the roads were also widened. The dome of the building was added some years later. A 'general shop' sold London newspapers that arrived by stage coach between 5pm and 6pm every day and also brought the mail.

Plate 11 Sketch of the Cornhill, Bridgwater
by John Chubb 1746-1818 Blake Museum

One would have witnessed a great procession of coaches entering and leaving the town each day, from early in the morning until late at night. To and fro through the South gate, along St Mary's Street, to the Cornhill, down Fore Street, over the bridge to Eastover and under the East gate. By the 1830s, Bridgwater coaching days had reached its peak. The coaches connected Bridgwater to Barnstaple in North Devon; Exeter in the south; and Bristol, Cheltenham and Birmingham in the north. They all had grand titles – The North Devon Telegraph, The Royal Devonshire, Estafette, Nonpareil, Exquisite, The Self-defence, Victoria, Speculator – to name just a handful. However, the pride of the town and the most famous was Swiftsure, which could reach London in 13 hours. The coach was 'well-horsed and well-equipped' and driven by a Mr Johns. It departed at 7.30am on Monday, Wednesday and Fridays from the Clarence Hotel in the Cornhill, arriving at Holborn at 9pm. It returned from London on Tuesdays, Thursdays and Saturdays. The route took it through Glastonbury, Wells, Shepton Mallet, Frome, Warminster, Amesbury, Andover and on to London.

The average coach could transport a total of 16 people along with the coachman and guard, four persons inside, the remainder on top outside. Imagine the scene – the fore boot and hind boot packed with small parcels, the roof piled high with luggage, just low enough to enable it to pass under the archways of the inns. There were boxes, carpet bags, gun cases and hampers belonging to the passengers inside and out, heaped up on the roof and hanging over the sides of the roof, the whole lot covered with a tarpaulin strapped down with leather straps. In addition baskets of game, hares and pheasants dangled from the lamp irons. Sometimes there was also a cradle underneath, which accommodated more items. No wonder these coaches frequently tipped over on their journeys resulting in injury and sometimes death. The roads were rough and in winter it could be very cold, and snow could make the journey hazardous. Passengers were often advised by friends to make a will before travelling!

Bridgwater's first newspaper was established in 1825 called the *Bridgwater and Somersetshire Herald*, which was later succeeded by *The Alfred* in 1831. In 1841 the railway arrived, linking Bridgwater to Bristol and thereby to London, while a year later there was also a line to Taunton. Down the centre of the high street was a row of old shops and stalls, locally known as 'The Shambles', dating back to medieval times, best known for their meat and fish. Eventually these were demolished in the early 1820s and new buildings erected including an Assize Hall, which went on to house the Grand Jury Room. The latter had previously occupied the old Guildhall in Fore Street and had been in a bad state of repair.

Although it was a hard working town with much poverty, there were social activities that people could enjoy. Tennis and fives were played in the 17th century and there had been a bowling green, while a cricket club was established in 1832. Oak Apple Day was celebrated each year and the Gunpowder Plot was commemorated annually by lighting 'squibs' and burning bonfires in the Cornhill. The actual carnival with floats, as we know it today, did not start until much later in the 19th century. Travelling players came to the town and by 1813 there was a theatre. The Bridgwater Races, which had been a popular event in the 18th century, were revived in 1813 and there was the annual St Matthew's Fair in September.

Alongside the many taverns there was a coffee house in Coffee House Lane (now Court Street); coffee houses in the 18th century were not how we imagine them today – somewhere to

Fig.5 Bridgwater Races 1794

pop into while out shopping or for meeting up with a friend for a chat. To start with, they were places of male preserve. Gentlemen paid one penny for a dish of coffee and met with fellow citizens to discuss the news, trade and politics of the day. Medical men, scientists and philosophers met and exchanged ideas – Sir William Blizard used to conduct consultations and give advice in the London coffee houses. In Bridgwater it is likely that the merchants in the town would meet there to conjure up business and the town apothecaries and surgeons would probably discuss cases – maybe Jonathan met colleagues there. By 1830 there was a reading room in the market house in the Cornhill and this later became the Literary and

Scientific Institution in 1840. By 1820 there were seven friendly societies in the town and these early insurance schemes were important in helping to fund health care and support people in times of need.

τ

So this was the bustling nature of Bridgwater town and its hard-working population. Jonathan completely embraced the life of the town and became its Mayor in 1824, but it was in the care of the sick that he invested his time and energies.

Chapter 4

The Art of Medicine

When a medical man enters a sick-room, he should keep his eyes and ears open, and avail himself of every hint which may enable him to form a correct judgment of his patient's case, and not disdain to weigh any suggestion which be offered conducive to his recovery, even though it may proceed from an unprofessional bye-stander.
Jonathan Toogood

At the beginning of the 19th century and for most of the 1800s the medical profession was still saddled with ancient theories of disease, handed down from the Greek physicians Hippocrates and Galen. Hippocrates (c.460-370 BC), now regarded as the Father of Medicine, lived on the Greek island of Cos off the coast of Turkey. He believed in the healing power of nature and practised a holistic and secular form of medicine – treatment should be designed to help the body to heal itself. He initiated what became the theory of the four humours – bodily fluids that are associated with a particular organ, namely phlegm with the brain; blood with the heart; yellow bile with the liver; and black bile with the spleen. The balance of these humours was believed to be essential for good health. For example, he hypothesised that epilepsy was due to a blockage (or build up) of phlegm in the brain. The various excretions of the body he interpreted as the body's natural defence mechanisms – phlegm, vomit, pus and diarrhoea were seen as the body getting rid of what was bad. Signs of illness were similarly interpreted – fever caused the skin to become flushed and the pulse rapid, indicating 'too much blood'. Therapy was therefore devised to help re-balance these humours mainly by diet, exercise, massage and blood-letting.

Galen (AD 129-c.210) was born in Pergamon, the Greek speaking part of the Roman Empire and, at that time, a wealthy town and intellectual centre. His father was an architect and the story goes that he had a dream in which the God of Healing (Aesclepius) visited him and told him that his son must become a physician. It took Galen 10 years to complete his training, studying at Alexandria in Egypt where he learned pharmacology, anatomy and surgery. Dissection of the human body was forbidden at this time and so this was undertaken on animals such as pigs and apes; he was only able to examine a human skeleton. At the age of 28 he became chief physician to the Roman gladiators, learning more about anatomy, wounds and surgery, and later was the personal physician to the Emperor Marcus Aurelius. He embraced humoralism, expanding the theory of the four humours and making it his own. This became the overriding basis of understanding disease. The four humours had by then been neatly correlated with various different constructs drawn from Natural Philosophy, namely the four seasons; the four ages of man; the four elements of Earth, Air, Fire and Water, as expressed in the four physical states of hot, dry, cold and wet (conditions observed in disease, such as shivering and sweating); and finally the four temperaments – sanguine, choleric, melancholic and phlegmatic (characteristics which were used as a guide to the susceptibility to certain diseases). The following diagram illustrates how all these components relate to each other. Similar interpretations of ill health remain the basis of other ancient forms of medicine – for example, practitioners of Chinese Medicine also aim to restore the body's balance.

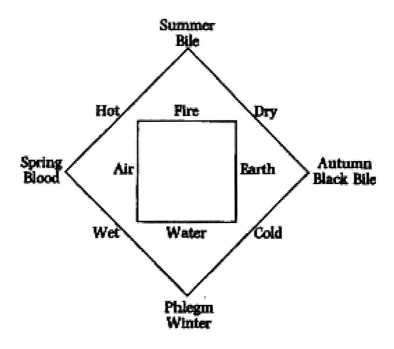

Fig.6 Diagram of the Four Humours

The writings of Galen spread throughout the western world and still remained an important part of the medical curriculum in the 18th and 19th centuries, despite the fact that some of his ideas had been proven to be incorrect. Andreas Versalius (1514-64), born in Brussels, became professor of anatomy and surgery at Padua University. Through his dissections of the human body he proved that Galen's understanding of human anatomy was in many ways inaccurate. For example, the liver did not have four or five lobes as seen in pigs! In 1628 the English physician William Harvey published his work on the circulation of blood – another blow to the followers of Galen. Humoralism, however, was adhered to, as there was no good alternative to the concept of disease until later studies in human physiology and the discovery of bacteria at the end of the 19th century.

τ

All this historical background was very pertinent to Jonathan Toogood. Although he was taught by eminent medical men of the time and hence exposed to what we would refer to as the cutting edge of medical science, his understanding of disease was fundamentally Galenic and he still referred to Hippocrates in his writings. He relied entirely on his five senses – sight, hearing, touch, smell and taste – to establish a diagnosis and this comes across in descriptions of his cases:

> '... the countenance was suffused, except about the nose and upper lip, which was preternaturally white; the eyes startled, and were glossy. There was an expression of anxiety amounting to agony. A quantity of mucus and saliva now collected constantly in the fauces [throat] and on the tongue, which protruded from the mouth in a hurried manner, and seemed anxious and impatient to have it removed ...The respiration became frequent; the hands and feet were cold and clammy; the pulse 160, and small...'

The above is part of a description of a boy with rabies. On another occasion, writing with hindsight, he describes a 55-year old man with a lung abscess (empyema): '...the pulse and respiration continued quick, with harassing cough; and it was evident that some latent mischief was going on in the chest; but as the use of the stethoscope was not known at this time, no positive conclusion could be formed as to its actual state'. The man continued to have night sweats and was losing strength: '...On making a careful examination, a puffiness was discovered at the lower edge of the right scapula (*shoulder blade*), which gradually increased for some days; and although the skin was not discoloured, and there was nothing pointing, there could be little doubt, that as the swelling became daily diffused, it contained fluid.' This in fact proved to be an abscess and it was treated accordingly.

These are just two examples of how important were his skills of observation. Of course, having made a diagnosis, treatment had to be undertaken and this again was still based on that of the Ancient Greeks. Attention to diet was high on the list, with such things as chicken broth, beef tea, tonics, wines and cordials commonly given and the patient was usually confined to bed. Procedures were then performed to rid the body of a build up of bad humours, thus restoring the balance. For example, if the patient was feverish, had obvious inflammation and a rapid pulse rate, it was thought that there was too much blood in the system and bleeding was recommended. Blood-letting was one of the mainstays of treatment and was used in a way that we would consider quite reckless and dangerous today – for example, women were frequently bled who were experiencing complications in childbirth, at a time when they would already have been weakened by blood loss; bleeding was often undertaken prior to surgery, or after a head injury or fracture!

There were several ways of bleeding the sick person – a lancet was used to cut into a vein, the blood draining into a bowl; or leeches were placed on the affected area in order to suck blood (the reason that medical men in the past were referred to as Leeches); or alternatively by cupping. For the latter the skin was scarified and then covered with a warmed, upside-down, glass cup, which would then draw the blood through the damaged skin.

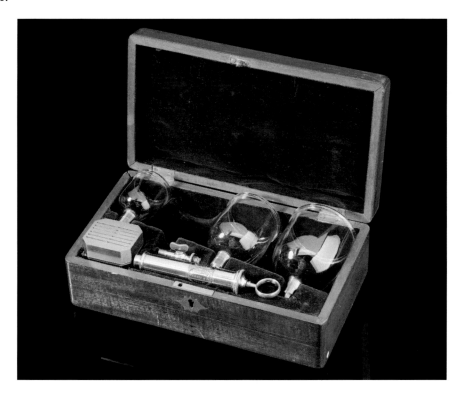

Plate 12 Cupping instruments
Wellcome Library

Jonathan learned from experience, however, that bleeding a patient could end badly and he became cautious in undertaking the procedure, commenting: 'I have always felt that, of all the remedies we employ, the lancet requires the greatest discrimination. I have witnessed the happiest effects from early and copious bleeding, and again, a total failure when pushed to a fearful extreme; and I have often regretted its too frequent employment'.

Purging was another way of removing offensive and poisonous substances from the body, and powerful emetics, laxatives and enemas (known as clysters) were employed for numerous conditions. Regular bowel movements became almost an obsession with the Victorians and lasted well into the twentieth century, probably as a result of this type of treatment.

Surgery could not be undertaken inside the body until the second half of the 19th century when ether and chloroform were introduced, and this will be discussed in the next chapter. A method therefore needed to be devised to treat more deep-seated problems and this became known as counter-irritation. This worked on the principle that a disturbance in an underlying organ could be counteracted by producing inflammation on the skin above that organ, which would then draw out the poison. This could be done with poultices, often made with bread and milk; or more alarmingly a blister was produced, either with a blister plaster which was impregnated with a chemical that irritated the skin, or by scolding the skin with boiling water or (worse) using a cautery iron to burn the skin. A variation of this was to make a small issue (cut) in the skin and to insert a small thread, known as a seton, to promote drainage of the pus. Alternatively horse beans (better known to us as broad beans) or peas could be inserted. Horse beans are rich in alkaloids, which are found in many plants that have medicinal properties such as the opium poppy. Jonathan favoured the use of counter-irritation and wrote about the method in the journals of the time. He tells of a young woman with a large lumbar abscess whom he had referred to Mr Abernethy in London, the latter advising the 'horse bean treatment'. The treatment took two years – certainly not a quick fix! Jonathan later remarked: 'She obtained a complete and lasting cure. She married shortly afterwards, and has since enjoyed uninterrupted health for more than thirty-five years'. Counter-irritation was still being used in the early part of the twentieth century, by which time the medical profession was exploring the underlying mechanism that made this treatment so successful.

Although voluntary hospitals had started to appear in the 18th century, they were only designed for the poor and were few in number. The vast majority of the population were looked after in their own homes when they were sick. Attention to environment was thought to be important and part of their treatment would involve good ventilation of the sick room. The overall belief was that 'bad air', known as miasma, was responsible for disease. Of course 'miasma' was everywhere! The streets were filthy with animal dung, sometimes even human excrement from overflowing cesspools. There were no public conveniences until the end of the nineteenth century and alleys were used by people wishing to relieve themselves. Mud was a constant feature, often mixed with household rubbish as well as waste from street markets and slaughter-houses. In London and other towns, the mud was black due to soot from coal fires. Soot was an ever-present feature in people's lives. Chimneys from houses and factories constantly puffed out smoke and there was the effluent from breweries and tanneries. The population of Britain was therefore exposed to an alarming cocktail of noxious effluvium and it is not surprising that they believed these to be a cause of ill health. An article, written in the *Provincial Medical & Surgical Journal* in 1844 about the effects of miasma by Dr John Smart, (a rural practitioner in Yorkshire, who in many instances had attended whole families 'prostrated' with a fever), stated: 'there is reason to suspect [the fever] arose from miasm, created by the decomposition of vegetable or animal matter.'

Sewage would drain into rivers, while water from water pumps was often contaminated by nearby privies. Burial grounds became overcrowded with often partially exposed bodies and the accompanying smell of rotting flesh. This was the case in St Mary's churchyard in Bridgwater in the 1840s and the nearby streets were badly affected. An article published in the *Bridgwater Times* in January 1848 described the interior of one of the houses: 'The pantry is close to the churchyard and instead of a window has an aperture of about eighteen inches square stuffed with hay. There is no privy to this house and no water on the premises. The smells of the new-dug graves are frequently very offensive'.

In 1846 there was a petition signed by the inhabitants of Worcester about the state of burial grounds: '...a space of ground totally inadequate to receive the remains of a large number of the dead, is in many instances productive of injury to the public health, owing to the noxious emanations from the soil'.

Nothing was known at the time about bacteria and viruses and the way water could become contaminated, causing epidemics such as cholera. Jonathan Toogood wrote to *The Alfred* newspaper on November 14th 1831 and again on August 6 1832 to warn the townspeople of impending risk of cholera, which was already breaking out in Bristol, Bath and Exeter (this was the first cholera pandemic to have reached Europe from the Indian sub-continent). He had even dispatched his son 'and partner' John Giles Toogood to Plymouth, where the cholera was 'violently raging', '...that he may be at the bedsides of the unhappy sufferers, acquire a practical knowledge of distinguishing symptoms and the most approved treatments'. On 16 January 1833 (according to Squibbs) Bridgwater observed a day of thanksgiving, having been happily spared the ravages of the disease. It was not until the end of the 19th century that Robert Koch (1843-1910) and Louis Pasteur (1822-1896) put forward their findings that became known as The Germ Theory, the latter paving the way for the pharmaceutical industry to develop new drugs and vaccines.

τ

The modern doctor's consulting room is very familiar to us with its couch, various medical instruments and the dominating computer screen! When Jonathan Toogood set up his practice in Bridgwater in 1806, he did not require a specially adapted room. Consultations would take place in his house or more often in the patient's home. He had no stethoscope, no ophthalmoscope, no laryngoscope, no otoscope – all this basic equipment plus instruments to measure blood pressure were still to be developed. His skill, as we have seen already, was in listening to

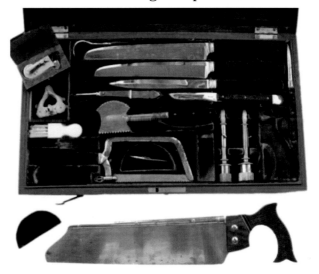

the patient's story along with careful examination. He would have been armed with a bag of surgical instruments similar to that shown in *Plate13 above*.

These were the tools needed for blood letting and for surgery. Jonathan would also keep a jar of leeches *(see Plate 14 below)*. When called in to see a sick child who was becoming comatose, he writes: 'Leeches were instantly applied to the temples.' Prescriptions would have been either prepared by himself or by the local apothecary at the druggist's store.

Plate 14 Leech jar
Wellcome Library

It is beyond the scope of this book to detail all the drugs Jonathan would have used at this time, and below is just a snapshot of a few. To help the reader, there is a glossary in the Appendix 1, which lists many of the preparations in common use at the time.

Opium, usually in the form of laudanum, was used for pain relief and as a sedative, quite often mixed with a wine such as Madeira. Digitalis, extracted from the foxglove plant, had been introduced in the late 18th century by William Withering for the treatment of dropsy (heart failure), but it was used cautiously by Jonathan, who understood the dangers of overdose, commenting: 'Digitalis ought in my opinion never to be given unless the practitioner sees his patient once, or better if twice daily, during its exhibition'. Many other drugs were derived from plants, but there were others that contained toxic chemicals such as arsenic, antimony and mercury, making use of their diuretic, emetic and purgative effects. Mercury was used extensively, often in the form of calomel (*mercurious chloride*) as a purgative, and it was the standard treatment for syphilis at this time.

τ

The stethoscope, still the most iconic item of the medical profession, did not arrive in Britain until the 1820s. It was viewed with suspicion by many – but not by Jonathan who embraced the instrument early on. Up until its introduction the body was effectively a closed book – only by actually putting an ear to the chest could some sounds be heard. This was not easy when it came to obese patients and it was deemed indelicate when examining the female sex.

Percussion (tapping) of the chest was used to help ascertain lung disease – a dull sound indicating fluid or consolidation (the latter a sign of pneumonia). The story of how this method of detection was discovered is a true example of lateral thinking. Leopold Auenbrugger (1722-1809), a Viennese physician, was the son of an innkeeper and used to see his father tapping the sides of the casks to determine how much beer or wine remained, the sound changing when he reached the level of the liquid. Auenbrugger found that by tapping (percussing) the body in different areas he could detect fluid and other signs of disease such as organ enlargement, and wrote a treatise about this form of examination in 1761. At a later date this was taken up by Jean-Nicolas Corvisart (1755-1821), Professor of Medicine in Paris, who went on to promote the method.

Palpation (feeling) could detect changes in the heart rhythm and heart murmurs and non-mediate auscultation – putting the ear to the chest wall, as we have already seen, could be difficult. It was a young physician and anatomist named René Laennec, working at the Necker Hospital in Paris in 1816, who devised the first stethoscope. This consisted of a cylinder of boxwood about 4cm diameter and 33cm long, perforated longitudinally by a narrow bore and hollowed out into a funnel shape at one end. Through this he could listen to the internal sounds of the body and matched these with the various diseases later detected at post-mortem, publishing his findings in 1818.

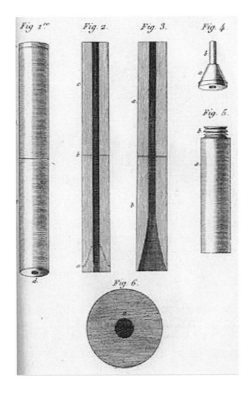

Fig.7 This first stethoscope was gradually modified and refined over the years to become the binaural instrument we know today
Wellcome Library

Medical practitioners who had undergone orthodox training like Jonathan Toogood were known as 'regulars' but they were not the only ones from whom the sick sought cures. Many a household owned 'self-help' guides such as a 'Family Herbal' and herbal remedies were handed down from generation to generation, as well as old superstitions. In the Bridgwater neighbourhood, Jonathan describes how the local people believed that medical men did not understand the nature or treatment of jaundice. They preferred to visit a village blacksmith who became renowned for curing the jaundice by making an incision on the top of the sufferer's head! Many of the country folk still believed in the 'white witch' that ruled over the levels, and many were in fear of this apparition and the 'evil eye'.

William Buchan, a Scottish physician, first published his famous self-help book *Domestic Medicine* in 1769, which contained advice on everything from pregnancy and childbirth to animal bites, and from venereal diseases to damp houses and beds. Many homes would have still owned a copy of this manual at the beginning of the 19th century *(Fig.8 below)*. Another popular booklet was *Every Man His Own Doctor* (or *A Cure of the Human Body*), published in 1835 (*Fig.9 below*).

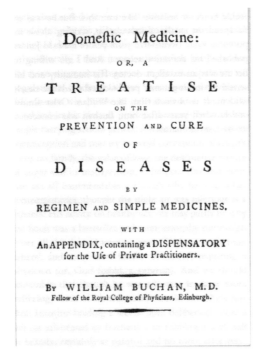

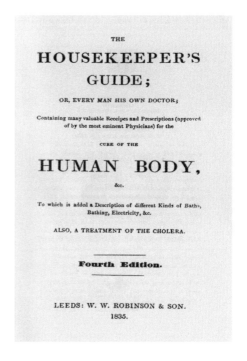

Fig.8 Buchan's Self-help book 1769   Fig.9 Self-help booklet 1835

A group of practitioners that had a profound influence on the sick were the 'irregulars', also known as quacks, itinerants, mountebanks and empirics. Consumerism came of age in the 18th century. With better incomes the middle classes were able to afford more luxuries and were seduced into buying various cures for their illnesses. The quacks (some of them trained medical men but the majority springing up from other trades) took advantage of this situation and, specialising in certain illnesses such as venereal diseases, travelled the country selling their remedies, known as nostrums. They were able to advertise their imminent arrival to a town in newspapers and by handbills, writing testimonials from satisfied customers and on occasion citing royal approval. They were showmen selling their wares – peddling not only remedies but also health elixirs, promoting good health and longevity. Product names were designed to attract the customer, using Latin or religious overtones such as Friar's Balsam. Many of their nostrums were similar to those used by the regulars and often contained mercury but, unlike the local surgeon-apothecaries, they would move on to the next town and were not responsible for the long-term care of the sick person, often leaving disaster in their wake.

The quacks benefited from the increase in hypochondria that had arisen in the 18th century and were able to make a good living selling their nostrums. In the 19th century they were given a new lease of life by the advent of the railway. Also mail order was becoming popular and a large amount of space was taken up in the newspapers to advertise their products, often as a 'cure for all'. In the *Bridgwater Times* Professor Holloway (not a real professor) described his Holloway's Pills as a 'Wonderful Medicine', which could be used in well over 30 diseases ranging from ague, asthma, and dropsy to tumours, female disorders and venereal infections. Another advertisement in the *Bridgwater & Somersetshire Herald* of February 16th 1831 recommended Dr. Bateman's Pectoral Drops for rheumatism, coughs, colds etc (*see fig.10 below*). Reputable medical men were concerned that people all too easily believed and trusted in these quack remedies, and that they were made very vulnerable by this type of advertising. The regular practitioner could offer much more than the travelling mountebank – examination, correct diagnosis and ongoing care, although the general public often preferred the magic elixir.

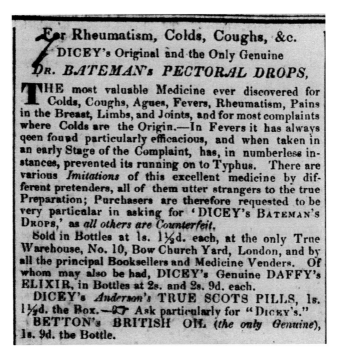

Fig.10 Advertisement for Dr Bateman's Drops

Not only were pills and potions sold to willing customers but the 18th century also saw the introduction of other alternative treatments including electricity, mesmerism (a type of hypnotism), hydropathy (water cures), and in the 19th century homeopathy. Jonathan deplored all quack treatments and when discussing the importance of humanity in the medical profession, he writes:

> 'Contrast this picture of the enlightened physician, with the bold, reckless, and dishonest empiric, who cruelly sports with the health and lives of those who are seduced by his artifices, and preys with rapacious avarice to the unfortunate valetudinarian and hypochondriac.'

Harsh words but, as we shall see in a later chapter (12), he was not averse to voicing his opinions on a range of medical matters but especially those regarding homeopathy.

The 19th century saw the practice of medicine evolve from an 'art' to a more scientific and hospital-based discipline. Surgery had started to flourish in the 18th century especially in London. Surgeons such as William Cheselden (1688-1752), who was famous for treating bladder stones, Percival Pott (1714-1789), John Hunter (1728-1793) and Henry Cline (1750-1827) all took centre stage. However, the 1800s were to see some momentous changes, which would have an enormous influence on the practice of surgery.

Chapter 5

General Practice, Surgery
and the advent of Anaesthesia

It is the duty of all who study the medical profession, to bring such observation as their experience has enabled them to collect into the general stock, the great object of medical science being the discovery of the best method of curing diseases, and mitigating those which the present imperfect knowledge of our art relieve only. Jonathan Toogood

General Practice in the 21st century differs a great deal from the work of the rural surgeon-apothecary at the beginning of the 19th century. The functioning of the human body has not changed, of course, and the pathologies associated with the various organs and systems remain the same, although some are a rarity now due to early detection and modern treatments. Bacteria, viruses and parasites (as in malaria) were unknown and hormones such as insulin were yet to be identified. The aetiology of disease was thought to be very different and treatments were developed that reflected this.

Like his modern counterpart, Jonathan Toogood would have been faced with a full case-load of medical conditions alongside surgical and midwifery emergencies, but unlike today's practitioners, he would have dealt with the majority of these entirely by himself in the patient's home, frequently making use of the kitchen table to undertake surgical procedures. He depended on his wit and knowledge, the latter acquired during his training and through ongoing access to medical books and journals.

As the number of medical practitioners increased in the late 18th and early 19th centuries, many turned to writing to share ideas and discoveries, these literary efforts being also a way of advancing their careers. Throughout history, treatises and textbooks have been written and there are famous medical papyri dating back to ancient Egypt. Most of these were written by the elite and were inaccessible to the majority before the development of the printing press. Privileged pupils, who undertook hospital training, were encouraged to record the cases and demonstrations they had seen. Jonathan would almost certainly have made copious notes and this was a habit that he continued throughout his life.

A number of societies sprang up in the second half of the 18th century; one of the first was The Lunar Society of Birmingham, established 1765, where learned men could meet and discuss scientific subjects. Among many distinguished members were the physicians Erasmus Darwin and William Withering, the potter Josiah Wedgwood, the engineer James Watt and the philosopher Joseph Priestley. Literary and Philosophical Societies that had started in Leeds, Liverpool and Manchester spread to other towns. Likewise Scientific and Medical Societies were springing up across the country – the Medical Society in Colchester, for example, was founded in 1784. Members of these societies were frequently physicians and surgeon-apothecaries, and the meetings provided an environment to discuss cases, exchange ideas and compare treatments. The Humane Society, established in 1774, was particularly concerned with resuscitation of the drowned.

Chester and Liverpool had Inoculation Societies, which were set up before Edward Jenner's work on cowpox and the introduction of the smallpox vaccination in 1798. Inoculation (later known as variolation) was introduced into Britain in 1721 by Lady Mary Wortley Montagu, the wife of the British Ambassador to Turkey, who had seen it used in Constantinople. It involved deliberate inoculation of smallpox material into the arm with the aim of causing a mild smallpox infection and thereby preventing a more serious infection by stimulating the body's own defences. In 1723 Caroline, the Princess of Wales had two of her children variolated. The procedure was not without risk as some people did develop the severe form of the disease and died. During 1721-28 there were 17 deaths from 858 variolations in Britain. Using cowpox instead of smallpox, as demonstrated by Jenner, proved to be just as effective but much safer.

The first Provincial Medical and Surgical Association was founded in Worcester, in 1832 by Charles Hastings, a provincial surgeon. These provincial associations sprang up across the country and Jonathan Toogood became a member of the Exeter Branch, attending meetings there as well as the annual 'Anniversary Meetings' held in London and other cities. In 1842 the tenth anniversary meeting was held in Exeter and Jonathan is recorded as one of the attendees.

Medical journals began to appear in the 19th century – the oldest in the UK was the *Edinburgh Medical Journal*, which started in 1805. *The Lancet* was founded by surgeon Thomas Wakley in 1823 and remains one of the foremost journals, publishing research articles and reviews, editorials, correspondence and book reviews. *The London Medical Gazette* followed in 1836 and in 1840 the Provincial Medical and Surgical Association started publishing its own journal. The Association later became known as the British Medical Association, which publishes the weekly *British Medical Journal*. These publications became an important way of disseminating information and allowed practitioners to make contacts and set up links across the country.

Jonathan tapped into this network, and it is through the archives of these journals that one can access his world. In 1853 he published a book entitled *Reminiscences of a Medical Life with Cases and Practical Illustrations (see Fig.11 overleaf)*. These writings have proved invaluable in order to understand his work and opinions at that time and are the source of many of the quotations used in this book.

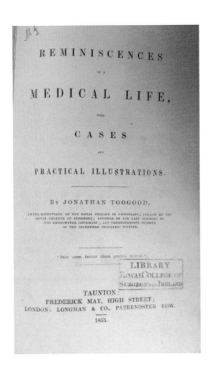

Fig.11 Jonathan Toogood's book *Reminiscences of a Medical Life* 1853
Author's copy

Every day Jonathan faced challenges to his intellect and knowledge. His patients, rich and poor, presented him with their numerous ailments, many of which he was ill equipped to remedy. Very often he could only ease symptoms and common infections often proved fatal, especially those in childhood such as diphtheria, scarlet fever and measles. On one occasion he comments about a farmer's wife whom he had treated for pneumonia: 'I am more inclined to attribute the success of the natural powers of her constitution, than to the judgment or skill of her medical adviser.'

Pulmonary Tuberculosis (phthisis) and the glandular presentation of the disease (scrofula) were a frequent diagnosis. In the 1840s it became quite popular to treat phthisis with cod-liver oil; Jonathan was a convert to this form of therapy and contributed to the *Provincial Medical Journal* with an article on his successes with its administration. These were inevitably anecdotal but a study was undertaken in 1848 at the Brompton Hospital for Consumption and Diseases of the Chest, which appeared to back up his own findings. This study was revisited in 2011 by Professor Malcolm Green, physician at the Royal Brompton Hospital, and although the study would not stand up to the rigours of drug trials today, it did show that the patients' general well-being improved. They gained weight and in some cases the disease was arrested; deterioration and death were shown to be lower in the group given cod-liver oil. Cod-liver oil contains Vitamin D and is now known to be involved in activating macrophages (part of the body's defence mechanism) to inhibit multiplication of the bacterium *Mycobacterium tuberculosis* (described by Koch in 1892), which is

37

responsible for tuberculosis. At the same time Vitamin D induces peptides (amino acids) that can destroy the mycobacteria. Cod-liver oil was also used to treat rickets and this is why it was given in childhood to help prevent this common and debilitating condition – it was still commonly administered for this purpose through much of the 20th century.

Heart conditions, such as dropsy, could be treated with digitalis and diuretics such as squill, a plant from southern Europe and north Africa, and copaiba, a resin obtained from a South American tree. Stroke, known as apoplexy, and other neurological conditions such as epilepsy were treated with the usual purging and bloodletting. Disturbances of the digestive tract would present frequently along with dysenteries. Venereal diseases were common as were various skin complaints, both often treated with mercury-based ointments. Typhus (also known as Gaol Fever), which was spread by body lice, was a constant problem in impoverished and overcrowded environments. The poor suffered from malnutrition and were often scorbutic.

Surgery was a branch of medicine that had started to make great strides in the 18th century and it was about to advance even more in the 1800s – first with the advent of anaesthesia in the 1840s and later with antisepsis. At the beginning of Jonathan's career these were still far in the future. In the absence of pain relief, speed was of the essence, but surgical procedures deep inside the body cavities could not be undertaken at all. The role of the surgeon was to treat and reunite fractures, attend to dislocated joints, remove superficial tumours, drain abscesses, cut for bladder stones, remove cataracts and on occasion perform mastectomies. The prognosis was very poor for breast cancer and surgery was rarely successful. Amputation was very much a last resort as it was associated with a high mortality rate due to complications such as haemorrhage and infection.

Accidents resulting in head injuries, fractures, dislocations and lacerations took up a considerable amount of Jonathan's time. These were frequently related to transport – people were thrown from horseback, wagons and carts, or run over by the same, and when the railway came to Bridgwater the workmen were often injured. No 'health and safety' in the 19th century! In the rural areas there were the inevitable farm accidents, and on one occasion Jonathan relates the story of a 15 year old lad who was 'knocked down by the vane of a windmill, which was rapidly revolving on a very windy day. The blow was so violent that it broke the wood-work of the frame, and drove the boy forwards to a considerable distance.' He had sustained a severe head injury and Jonathan considered the case hopeless, but despite this he removed a total of sixteen pieces of bone from the shattered skull and the young patient made a full recovery. The docks in Bridgwater proved to be another hotbed of accidents. Jonathan was called to treat a youth of 18, who had suffered severe injuries of both legs due to entanglement in a rope that was attached to a steam-tug towing a vessel up the river. Initially the boy's friends and family refused amputation, despite the lad's consent, but the wounds turned gangrenous and amputation was his only chance of recovery, so this was eventually undertaken.

Amputation in a case of spreading gangrene had always been frowned upon, and the unfortunate person was left to their fate. Jonathan Toogood was not afraid to buck the trend and agreed with Dominique-Jean Larrey (1766-1842), the great French military surgeon who was engaged in the Napoleonic Wars and performed hundreds of amputations on traumatic wounds. Larrey – Jonathan mentions him several times in his writings – is remembered for his organisational skills in the field and insisted on his teams of surgeons working near the frontline so that surgery could be undertaken quickly. He also designed the 'flying ambulance', a light horse-drawn vehicle used to convey the injured soldier away from the battlefield. Many of his ideas remain the basis of military surgery even today. Jonathan confessed 'that it has always appeared to me better to offer the patient the chance, which a doubtful operation would afford, than leave him to a certain death' and was not afraid to recommend such ideas to his colleagues.

Another surgical problem, common at that time, was popliteal aneurysm. This is a dilatation of the popliteal artery, the latter traverses the popliteal fossa which is situated at the back of the knee. This was frequently seen in horse-riders and coachmen and may have been caused by pressure from their riding boots. John Hunter (1728-1793), father of modern scientific surgery, developed a method of tying off the femoral artery (the main artery in the thigh which becomes the popliteal artery) to treat this condition. Jonathan practised this method commenting: 'I have tied the artery, and assisted others many times in popliteal aneurism, without a single instance of failure, and I greatly prefer this simple and safe operation, which is attended with infinitely less pain, trouble and anxiety, to the clumsy, tedious, and uncertain treatment of compression.'

Rhinoplasty, a procedure to restore an injured nose, dates back centuries. Jonathan's nephew by marriage (John Allen Giles) recalls in his diary how he watched his uncle in 1824 'make a new nose for a man from the skin of his forehead.' In the Wellcome Library in London are two drawings by Jonathan showing the hand of a boy of sixteen. In the first there is an obvious tumour at the base of the ring finger, and in the second the tumour has been excised along with the finger *See plate 15 below.* He describes the removal of the tumour in his book, commenting that it 'had grown to such a size as not only to render the finger useless, but to impede very considerably the motions of the hand.' After surgery the wound healed quickly with a favourable outcome – 'He had a useful hand with very little deformity.' *See plate 16 overleaf.*

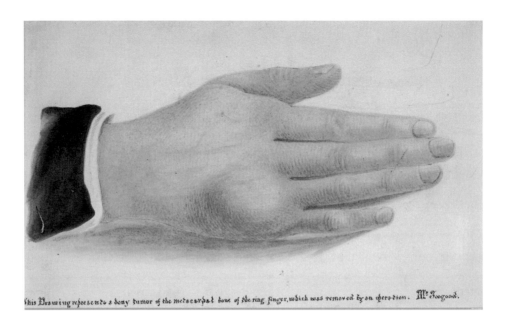

This Drawing represents a bony tumor of the metacarpal bone of the ring finger, which was removed by an operation. Mr Toogood.

Plate 15 illustration of 'pre-op' hand tumour *Wellcome Library*

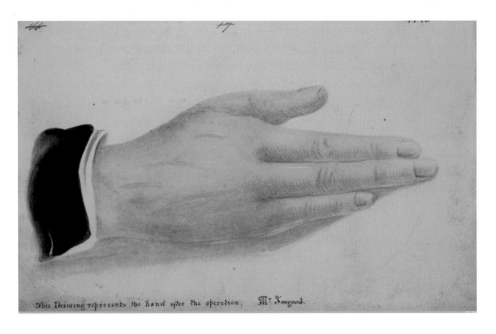

This Drawing represents the hand after the operation. Mr Toogood.

Plate 16 illustration of 'post-op' hand tumour *Wellcome Library*

There is no doubt that surgery in the 19th century was becoming more sophisticated and the introduction of anaesthesia opened up another chapter for this speciality.

τ

Throughout the centuries the relief of pain in surgery remained an enigma that hindered the progress of this branch of medicine. Surgery had to be quick and the surgeons of the 18th and early 19th centuries prided themselves on their speed when undertaking certain procedures. Surgery within the body cavities, apart from one or two brave exceptions, could not be tolerated by patients and, if attempted, would usually result in death either during the operation, caused by haemorrhage and shock, or later from sepsis. Alcohol and opium were frequently used to dull the pain but restraint was nearly always required to keep the patient from struggling. Fanny Burney, the English novelist (1752-1840), wrote a very moving account of the agony she experienced in 1811 when undergoing a mastectomy performed by Dr Larrey in Paris. Her words are very chilling and harrowing to read but they do give the reader a real insight into what it was like to be 'under the knife' at this time.

Among other methods tried was a form of hypnotism known as mesmerism, named after Franz Mesmer (1734-1815), an Austrian doctor, who believed in animal magnetism and was able to put his patients into a type of a trance. Unfortunately it did not prove to be successful as a form of anaesthesia.

The gas nitrous oxide had been discovered by Joseph Priestley in 1772 but it was the chemist Humphrey Davy (1778-1829) who described its euphoric and analgesic effects in 1800. Nicknamed 'laughing gas' it was used for party frolics, although an enterprising dentist in America Horace Wells (1815-1848) employed it for dental extractions. His former partner William Morton (1819-1868) in 1845 recommended its use to surgeons at the Massachusetts General Hospital, but when Wells came to demonstrate its use, it failed and he was ridiculed. It took many more years before nitrous oxide was employed in anaesthesia.

Ether had first been prepared in 1540 and likewise had been used in party frolics. William Morton found liquid ether useful in deadening the pain in tooth sockets after an extraction, and tried the effects of inhaling the vapour on himself, a dog and his assistants. A surgeon, hearing of these experiments, introduced Morton to John Collins Warren (1778-1856), professor of surgery at Massachusetts General Hospital. He agreed to use it on a young man who required surgery on a neck tumour and was terrified at the prospect. The operation on October 16th 1846 lasted 30 minutes and was completely pain free.

News travelled rapidly across the Atlantic and in December of the same year Robert Liston (1794-1847), Professor of Surgery at University College Hospital agreed to use ether to perform an amputation. The successful use of anaesthesia to prevent the pain of surgery spread throughout the United Kingdom and across the Channel to Paris, and went on to be used during the Crimean War (1853-1856).

Jonathan embraced this new form of pain relief and describes its use in a patient who had a dislocation of the ankle joint: 'She was put under the influence of ether, and the bone replaced without difficulty'.

Chapter 6

Childbirth and the Cheshire Cat

The safety, nay, the life of the patient, depends on the care, experience, and watchfulness, of the attending practitioner   Jonathan Toogood

By the early part of the 19th century the 'man-midwife' had come of age and there was an expectation that the surgeon-apothecary would be present at childbirth alongside a nurse and female members of the family. There was, however, no formal training in midwifery and many of the surgeons were as ignorant as the 'nurses' they rebuked, despite the fact that these women often had many years of experience and knowledge, handed down through the generations. Jonathan recognised that the practice of midwifery needed a great deal of skill and 'involves duties of too responsible and dangerous a nature to be entrusted to ignorant women and nurses. All men do not possess the necessary qualifications, and are not equally adapted for it'.

Childbirth was extremely hazardous at this time and maternal mortality was high. Between 1800 and 1850 the rate was 5 per 1,000 live births, compared with today's figure for the United Kingdom of 1 per 10,000. Many members of the medical profession held the practice of midwifery in low esteem – Jonathan made the comment that they considered it 'too unimportant a branch of medicine to engage the attention of scientific men, who contend that the practice is degrading, and ought to be left to old women and nurses.' He went on to say: 'it appears to me that the careful study of this branch of our art is absolutely necessary to avoid the mischief of "meddlesome midwifery," than which nothing can be worse.'

Jonathan was not alone in making disparaging remarks about the women acting as midwives. Samuel White, a surgeon from Bicknoller near Taunton, wrote a letter to *The Lancet* in January 1852 commenting on the desire of the Royal Colleges for medical practitioners to have a diploma in midwifery (part of the call for Medical Reform at that time) 'whilst hundreds of the most illiterate and grossly ignorant women are allowed to practise the obstetric art with the greatest impunity, without the least interference of the authorities'. He believed them to be 'the greatest danger to the labouring classes' and not content with this, he states: 'In rural districts, the confinements are chiefly monopolized by a set of superannuated old women, whose skill lies chiefly in taking snuff, drinking gin and tea and the midwife's half-crown fee'.

This is the image Charles Dickens portrayed in his character Sairey Gamp, the drunken nurse in *Martin Chuzzlewit*. In his defence, Samuel White expressed a desire that they should be qualified and that he had no objection to this: 'glad, indeed, should I be to relinquish all midwifery; I have had enough travelling over a rugged, hilly country, fording of brooks,

&c., during the nights of a dreary winter'. It is unknown whether Jonathan would have agreed with his colleague's views about the training of female midwives, but there is no evidence that he wished to give up midwifery, which he considered an important part of his practice.

Jonathan's nephew by marriage (John Allen Giles) wrote in his memoirs about his uncle attending his mother in one of her confinements at Southwick House, when 'the snow was lying deep' in the winter of 1812-1813. He remembers him coming in his carriage with two horses, unfortunately driving into a ditch, describing the latter as a small river – eight feet in width and very deep. This appeared not to deter Jonathan as he continued to practise midwifery over the next three decades.

τ

During his time at St Bartholomew's Hospital, Jonathan had attended the lectures of Dr. John Clarke (1758-1815). A pupil of John Hunter at St George's Hospital, John Clarke soon developed a busy obstetric practice in Chancery Lane. He became known for his kindness and gentleness towards his patients and was well respected as a teacher. He became an authority on difficult midwifery cases; his first publication was on puerperal fever and he was interested in nausea associated with pregnancy. In 1803 he wrote a successful textbook *The London Practice of Midwifery*, which also contained a section on diseases of children, and it would be nice to think that Jonathan owned a copy. Later in his life Dr. Clarke concentrated on gynaecology and paediatrics, the latter did not become a separate speciality till later in the 19th century. He became one of ten licentiates in midwifery created by the College of Physicians but was actually very critical of the College's attitude towards midwifery and diseases of children.

Jonathan refers to John Clarke's lectures in his writings and it is obvious that he held him in high regard. When discussing the use of obstetric forceps, he comments: 'I have always used the short forceps recommended by the late Dr. John Clarke, and by attending to the directions so clearly laid down in his lectures, never experienced any difficulty in applying them.'

Fig.12 Haighton's Obstetrical forceps, 1790.
Wellcome Library

It was not until 1841 that the Royal College of Surgeons introduced a separate midwifery exam and in 1844 offered a Diploma, which was already compulsory in Edinburgh and Europe at this stage. It took another 40 years (1886) before it was a requirement for a midwifery qualification to be listed in the Medical Register.

The four main causes of maternal death in the 19th century were puerperal fever (often referred to as 'childbed fever'), haemorrhage, convulsions and illegal abortion. Jonathan describes in some detail his management of such cases.

τ

Puerperal fever, described by some as a 'lamentable disease', and 'that plague of the lying-in chamber', was untreatable before the age of antibiotics. The usual treatment was bloodletting and purging but in nearly all cases the woman would perish due to the infection. In the first half of the 19th century there were many theories about its origin but some astute practitioners linked the fever with an infection of the skin known as erysipelas. The idea that there was a factor being transferred to women by their doctors and midwives, was put forward by Dr. Alexander Gordon (1752-1799) in 1790 in Aberdeen, but he was criticised by his contemporaries. Similarly Oliver Wendell-Holmes (1809-1894), Professor of Anatomy in Boston USA, was vilified when he published his essay *Contagiousness of Puerperal Fever* in 1843, in which he described a study of cases on either side of the Atlantic, convincingly showing that these cases of puerperal fever were transmitted by some form of 'contagion' rather than a product of miasma. He linked such cases to medical practitioners performing post-mortem examinations on women who had died of puerperal fever, just prior to attending women in childbirth. Furthermore he demonstrated how the disease was transmitted to patients by their attendants, who had been in contact with cases of childbed fever or erysipelas without washing their hands or changing their outer clothes before moving on to the next patient. Professor Wendell-Holmes laid out clear guidelines on how to take precautions to reduce transfer – these included 'thorough ablution and change of every article of dress' after undertaking autopsies and allowing 24 hours before attending a midwifery case. He also recommended that practitioners who have dealt with a case of puerperal fever should allow at least a month to elapse before attending the next woman in labour.

About the same time Dr Ignaz Semmelweiss (1818-1865) in Vienna had made a similar connection with puerperal fever and the transfer of 'cadaveric matter' and published a book entitled *The Aetiology of Childbed Fever* in 1858. He proposed scrubbing of hands with solutions of chloride of lime before visiting the lying-in wards. He too experienced criticism from the medical establishment. It was not until much later in the century that the bacterium *Streptococcus* was identified as the causative organism in puerperal fever and erysipelas.

Haemorrhages, both ante-partum and post-partum, were another potential killer and could often go undetected for a period of time after a normal

44

delivery. Jonathan Toogood was very aware of this complication and comments: 'Uterine haemorrhage is more frequent, more embarrassing, and more dangerous than any other accident in the practice of midwifery', and goes on to advise due diligence.

Convulsions due to pre-eclampsia, often referred to as toxaemia, were difficult to treat. There was no means of measuring blood pressure at this time and although there were reports of the condition being linked with protein in the urine, there was little understanding of the aetiology. If the woman perished, the cause of death was generally thought to be due to disease of the kidneys.

Obstructed delivery causing a protracted labour was another frequently insurmountable problem. Mal-presentation of the child could often be resolved by turning the baby in the womb, but many women had a contracted pelvis, either due to injury, congenital malformation or deformity as a result of rickets. Although there was the occasional report of a successful Caesarian section, this would usually result in the death of the mother and would only be performed to save the child if the mother had already succumbed. All attempts were made to save the woman and this would often result in a procedure known as craniotomy, where the child was destroyed and removed from the uterus in pieces. Jonathan reports that when he first started to practise in Bridgwater, he found to his 'astonishment' that this method had been resorted to in all cases of difficulty and that the forceps had never been applied, and admits when he was a young practitioner that it was an error he 'fell into'.

τ

Anaesthesia and antisepsis, which were introduced later in the 19th century, brought in a new era of obstetric management and gradually childbirth became safer. James Young Simpson (1811-1870), Professor of Midwifery in Edinburgh, was the first to use ether in his obstetric practice in January 1847. However, it was slow to take effect, often associated with coughing and vomiting and it was highly inflammable. He therefore experimented with other drugs, trying them on himself and his two assistants! He found chloroform to have many advantages over ether and by the end of 1847 reported on its use in obstetric cases:

> 'I have employed it, with few exceptions, in every case of labour that I have attended, and with delightful results, and I have no doubt whatever that some years hence the practice will be general.'

Plate 17 James Young Simpson (1811-70)

Jonathan knew Professor Simpson and makes the following observation in his book: 'The discovery of vaccination by Jenner, which has saved hundreds of thousands from this loathsome disease; and more recently, that of the use of chloroform, by my friend Dr Simpson, which so completely annuls human suffering, must be ranked amongst the greatest blessings of mankind.'

Not everyone in the profession agreed with this sentiment. An article, published in June 1847 in the *Provincial Medical and Surgical Journal* and entitled 'Injurious Effects of the Inhalation of Ether', was very critical of the use of anaesthesia and goes on to say:

> 'Pain during operations is, in the majority of cases, even desirable; its prevention or annihilation is, for the most part, hazardous to the patient. In the lying-in chamber nothing is more true than this: pain is the mother's safety, its absence her destruction. Yet are those bold enough to administer the vapour of ether even at this critical juncture, forgetting it has been ordered [in religious scripture] that "in sorrow shall she bring forth.'

The author of this comment was not alone in his opinions. But when Queen Victoria chose to have chloroform at the birth of her eighth child in 1853, many of these views were swept away as more and more women requested pain relief.

In the first seven years in his practice, Jonathan attended 1,135 midwifery cases, most of which he describes as natural labours. He went on to practise midwifery for over 40 years, and the following two quotations from his book give us some insight as to the amount of time and dedication he showed to this aspect of his work. Describing the qualities a medical man should possess:

'He will be best fitted for the arduous task who possesses a good constitution, is capable of enduring great fatigue, and patiently submitting to many privations, and without rashness, with sound judgment and firm determination, which he will often be required to exercise when exhausted by long watching and anxiety; in addition to which, if his manner is kind and his disposition cheerful, the practice will be more agreeable to himself and his patients.'

'How important then is the study of midwifery; an imperfect knowledge of its practical part may lead to the most deplorable consequences, where error of the head or hand may suddenly bereave a fond husband of a beloved wife, children of a tender and affectionate mother, and plunge a whole family into grief, and probably, ruin.'

Gynaecology was in its infancy at the start of the 19th century, and was not a separate speciality, the surgeons of the day attending to uterine prolapse and tumours alongside ovarian tumours and cysts. Trauma following childbirth was a frequent problem, often resulting in a fistula (opening) between the bladder and vagina which resulted in very distressing symptoms for the woman such as incontinence. Jonathan also saw his fair share of accidental passage of female catheters into the bladder. On one occasion he requested the opinion of Sir Astley Cooper who wrote back with a description of how the catheter should be removed. Sir Astley showed Jonathan a drawing of a calculus, formed over a catheter that he had retrieved from a bladder 'by the usual operation, some years since, at Guy's Hospital.'

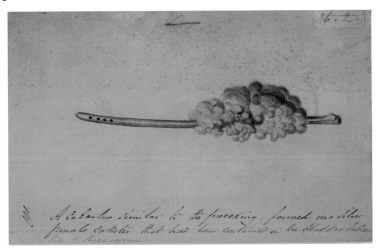

Fig.13 Sir Astley Cooper's drawing of a calculus
formed around a catheter   *Wellcome Library*

Menstrual disorders were common, menorrhagia (heavy periods) frequently resulting in iron deficiency anaemia. In his book Jonathan devoted a separate chapter entitled *On the Physical Development of Young Females*, in which he discusses a condition known as Chlorosis. This disease affected young women (it was only rarely diagnosed in young men) and was common from the sixteenth century until the 1920s, and is known by several aphorisms – 'green sickness', 'the virgin's disease' and a disorder due to 'unrequited love'. It affected all social classes and its main clinical features included menstrual disorder, disturbance of appetite, an altered mental state and 'pica', the latter referring to eating indigestible materials such as chalk or cinders. The skin colour was often referred to as very pale with a greenish tinge, although this was debatable. I.S.L Louden, a research associate at the Wellcome Unit for the History of Medicine at Oxford University, writing in the *British Medical Journal* in 1980, put forward the theory that Chlorosis is closely linked to Anorexia Nervosa, a 'modern disorder', or that quite possibly they are one and the same illness. He proposed that the condition could be split into four phases: up to 1750 when it was described as due to 'love-sickness'; from 1750-1850 it was believed to be a uterine disorder; from 1850 it was considered a form of anaemia; and the final phase, from 1900-1920, he describes as 'the "Cheshire Cat" phase' when Chlorosis completely disappeared! Other causes such as tight corsetry or hookworm infestation have also been postulated. Whatever the cause, it was of real concern to the practitioners in the 19th century and involved a great deal of their time. Jonathan comments: 'The slightest deviation from the natural state, in young females, should not be allowed to pass unnoticed; for if it be true that prevention is better than remedy, it is undeniably so in such cases.'

Fig.14 Engraving of
woman with Chlorosis
Wellcome Library

The workload of the 19th century practitioner with all the accompanying difficulties was enormous and the treatment of all ailments took place in patients' homes, often in quite unsuitable, insanitary conditions. By the end of the 18th century voluntary hospitals were starting to become established in the larger towns and Jonathan was determined to provide a similar system of care in the town of Bridgwater.

Chapter 7

Bridgwater Infirmary

'The poor are my best patients, for God is their paymaster'
Herman Boerhaave (1668-1738)

Hospitals are institutions that we very much take for granted in the western world, with their up to date technology, wards, operating theatres, professionally trained medical and nursing staff, accident and emergency and outpatient departments – not forgetting all the other medical professionals, such as physiotherapists, occupational therapists and radiographers that make up the modern hospital team, working alongside the medical staff in their chosen speciality. This certainly was not the case 200 years ago. Jonathan Toogood had to attend to his patients, rich and poor, in their own homes, because the original medieval provision for the sick had been dismantled long ago and had not been replaced.

Like many towns in medieval England, Bridgwater had a leper hospital known as the Hospital of St Giles, which was situated just outside the old west gate from the middle of the 14th century until 1539. Leprosy had appeared in Britain in the 4th century AD and by 1044 it was becoming a significant social problem. Sufferers were forced to withdraw from society and as a consequence small leper houses started to appear.

In 1213 an Augustine Priory was founded and became known as St John's Hospital. It was built in 1216 by William Brewer at the eastern end of Eastover and gradually expanded to include a church, chapter house, parlour, cloister and gardens. Medieval hospitals were established to give charity to the poor, sick, and to travellers. Although they cared for the sick by providing a bed, clean linen and nourishing food, their main priority was the soul of the poor person, ensuring their salvation. Inmates were expected to attend the chapel to worship alongside the brothers and sisters. The infirmaries were frequently combined with the chapels, so that the bedridden could participate in the masses. Hospitals varied in the type of people they were allowed to admit – St John Bridgwater forbade lepers, lunatics, persons suffering from 'falling sickness' (epileptics), contagious diseases, pregnant women, suckling infants or any 'intolerable person', but not all hospitals were quite so discriminating. In time St John Bridgwater became one of the richest hospitals in the country with an income of £120 per annum in 1535, being largely financed by tithes from the local church and eight other churches in Cornwall, Devon and Somerset. It became very unpopular in the town, as it was in competition with the local parish church and was viewed as serving its own interests rather than those of the sick.

A Franciscan Friary was founded in 1245 and occupied the area adjacent to Friarn Street in Bridgwater. The monks would also attend to the sick, frequently visiting people in their own homes. These facilities for the poor and infirm came to an abrupt end with the Reformation and the subsequent dissolution of the monasteries. The Friary surrendered in 1538 and St John Bridgwater hospital itself terminated in 1539. Apart from a few almshouses and a small workhouse for the elderly and sick paupers, there were no other institutions in Bridgwater for the care of the sick until the beginning of the 19th century.

τ

Georgian England was to witness an epidemic of hospital building across the country and by 1800 many large towns congratulated themselves on the establishment of a new infirmary. In the South West the following hospitals were established in the 18th century – Bristol in 1737, Bath in 1742 and Exeter in 1741. These hospitals were charities, founded in an era of philanthropy and became known as Voluntary Hospitals, funded by goodwill and generosity and run by volunteers, governors and trustees and honorary medical staff. They were intended for the deserving or 'labouring' poor and were frequently founded by civic worthies – medical men were not necessarily the driving agents. Unlike the old medieval hospitals, the new hospitals were secular and their main aim was to cure or relieve sickness; they were not meant for the terminally ill. In theory outright paupers were not supposed to be admitted and would be 'cared for' in small workhouses, although in practice there is evidence that they were often treated in the voluntary hospitals, especially if they required surgery or needed emergency treatment.

Jonathan was well aware of the formation of these hospitals around the country and, of course, had completed his own surgical training in a hospital surrounded by the latest equipment and alongside industrious surgeons with innovative ideas. He recognised that rural surgeons had many disadvantages and experienced considerable difficulties, with which the metropolitan surgeons did not have to contend. In a hospital setting there were other competent assistants to call on for advice, but in the countryside a surgeon 'must accept of such assistance as is within his reach, and is often placed in the difficult position of choosing between a rival who watches him with unfriendly eyes, or one on whom he is quite aware that he cannot depend on an emergency, or unforeseen difficulty.' This is a revealing insight into the competition between practitioners at this time and also into their levels of competence.

He graphically describes two situations that illustrate very well the type of difficulties that came his way:

> 'On one occasion, I was called on to tie the inguinal artery, in a case of aneurism of the popliteal, the whole limb being enlarged as to admit of no other course, on a rickety table, hardly strong enough to support the weight of the patient, in a small room, admitting very little light; and in another case, where both legs were broken by a loaded wagon passing over them, it was necessary to remove the patient into the door-way of the cottage, to obtain sufficient light by which to amputate.'

It was frequent events such as these that convinced Jonathan that Bridgwater needed an infirmary. He encouraged his medical colleagues in the town to help provide such an establishment, although he admits the idea was not without opposition and difficulties. There was a mixed picture of institutional provision in Somerset. Bath Hospital was already well established but was miles away from Bridgwater, requiring a very difficult journey for the seriously ill. Closer to home, Jonathan was aware of the small, successful dispensary and infirmary, set up in Wiveliscombe in 1804, and would use this as a prototype.

Wiveliscombe is a small market town on the Devon and Somerset border at the foot of the Brendon Hills, about 9 miles west of Taunton and roughly 16 miles from Bridgwater as the crow flies. Its dispensary-cum-infirmary was the inspiration of Dr Henry Sully, a well-established medical practitioner in the town and by all accounts quite a character. He became surgeon to the Duke of Cumberland (son of George III), who later became the King of Hanover. With the backing of the Hancock family, who were rich bankers, Dr Sully opened the Wiveliscombe dispensary in 1804 with his partner Mr Bishop Cranmer. The dispensary was designed for servants, apprentices, labourers and mechanics and was funded by donations, legacies and subscriptions. It proved to be very successful. In the year 1815 from January to December, 724 patients were admitted to the dispensary and annual subscriptions were running between £400 and £500 in the years up to 1815. By 1822 there were 12 beds and patients would even come from distant parts of both Somerset and Devon.

Plates 18,19 Wiveliscombe Dispensary and Infirmary 1804
author's photos

Taunton, on the other hand, had its setbacks. Plans for a county hospital had been originally drawn up for the town in 1772 and the building of the hospital actually started. Unfortunately the project failed, probably because it was over ambitious and ran into financial problems. Potential backers were perhaps more interested in investing in the silk industry, an important trade in the town at the time. In 1793 the unfinished and dilapidated building was sold to clear the debt and was then converted into a private residence by one of the town's medical practitioners Mr J. Bryant. Later it became a convent and was eventually incorporated into King's College school. A dispensary for 'the relief of the indigent sick' was opened in 1789 by Dr Cox and carried on by him and by Mr H. Trott, a surgeon, at his own expense. By 1793 this had also failed and was closed in August of that year. It was not until 1809 that Dr Malachi Blake proposed the building of a hospital, managing to get his fellow medical colleagues in the town to support his proposal. The opening and success of the Wiveliscombe Infirmary is thought to have acted as an incentive. This time the plans for the building in East Reach were more modest and the hospital opened its doors to patients in 1812.

τ

On the 26th June 1813 a general public meeting was held at the Grand Jury Room in Bridgwater. This was an 18th century colonnaded building in the High Street used for quarter sessions, but when the judges and magistrates were not residing over the court, the building was used to store wool, flax, hides and tallow. It was demolished in 1856. The meeting was attended by a large number of notable residents of the town and the surrounding neighbourhood. The Mayor of Bridgwater, Mr James Mills, chaired the meeting. Fifteen resolutions were unanimously adopted and recorded in the minutes, the first of which set out the purpose of establishing a medical institution in the town – 'for the relief of the labouring poor (requiring medical and surgical assistance) in that and the neighbouring parishes.' The institution was to be 'under the direction of a Committee of Management,' which was subject to the regulations set out in the minutes. Sir Philip Hales, Baronet, accepted the office of President for the year, while 22 gentlemen from the town and neighbourhood were appointed members of the committee, with John Chubb as Treasurer and Mr Morley Chubb as Honorary Secretary. Dr Dunning (*see Plate 21 overleaf*) and Dr Haviland agreed to act as physicians; Messrs. John Symes, John Haviland and William Anstice to be consulting surgeons; and Messrs. Jonathan Toogood, Henry Axford, Haviland, and Stradling to act as surgeons to the institution. Mr Henry Axford also agreed to officiate as the institute's apothecary.

Plate 20 Dr John
Dunning
Blake Museum

It was also laid down that the President, Physicians and Surgeons would remain permanent members of the management committee, along with any members who donated 20 guineas or more (including the equivalent in land). Those who subscribed 5 guineas or more annually, or made an initial donation of 5 guineas and then subscribed 2 guineas or more annually, could also continue to be members as long as their subscriptions were kept up. As pointed out earlier in this chapter, donations and subscribers were fundamental to such voluntary organisations. Subscribers were entitled to recommend patients to the institution and the number they were allowed to refer depended on the amount of annual subscription paid – one guinea entitled a subscriber to refer 4 out-patients; 2 guineas allowed one in-patient and 2 out-patients or a total of 6 out-patients; and so on in proportion to the annual subscription paid. These were the usual arrangements at the time and were the same at both Wiveliscombe and Taunton.

Finally, at this first meeting, it was agreed that no in-patient was to be admitted 'without bringing a security from some substantial person to defray the expense of his removal or burial in case he die', and that an in-patient 'also pay the nurse 5s 6d per week for his board unless he chose to board himself'. Again this was in keeping with the other voluntary hospitals of that time, and although the hospitals were designed to cure or relieve symptoms, patients inevitably did die on occasions and the establishments did not have enough income to take on funeral expenses as well.

On Tuesday 6th July 1813 another meeting was held in the Town Hall, which Jonathan attended, when further rules for in-patients were adopted.

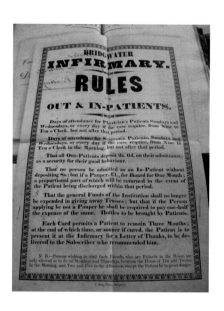

Plate 21 Later version of Infirmary rules 1838
Somerset Heritage Centre

In-patients were to be admitted on Sunday mornings between 7am and 10am, and at no other time except in the case of an emergency. The patient was to attend with a letter of recommendation obtained from a benefactor or subscriber. One wonders how easy it was for some patients to obtain such a letter, but there were a number of clergymen who were subscribers and many patients would have been referred by the medical practitioners themselves. Unfortunately the author has not been able to find a copy of one of these letters pertaining to Bridgwater Infirmary. However, below are two examples of recommendation cards used by Wiveliscombe and Taunton Hospitals respectively, which are quite likely to be very similar to those used at Bridgwater:

I recommend _____ of the Parish of _____ knowing _____ to be a proper object of this institution and have directed _____ to observe the rules printed on the back of this card. _____ day of _____ 18___.

_____ Subscriber

To the Committee of the Taunton and Somerset Hospital.
Gentlemen,
I recommend A.B. of the Parish of _____ to be admitted a Patient of the said Hospital, and whom I believe to be a proper object of your charity. I remain, etc

It disturbs our modern sensibilities to read that patients were referred to as objects of the charity but, of course, it was just that – a charity for the deserving poor and it was important that the institution was not misused.

Admission was restricted to those in most need, and many patients were simply given advice and medicine and not admitted. They were also obliged to bring along their own phials and gallipots in which the medicines were dispensed. If admitted, the patient was required to bring their own bed linen and clothes and be responsible for their own washing. Stay in hospital could be very protracted, but if longer than three months, the letter of recommendation had to be renewed and the person considered as a new patient.

Out-patients were to attend on the mornings and hours appointed by their surgeon or physician, and had to pay a deposit of 2s 6d which would be returned when they were discharged; but if they failed to attend the appointment, their half crown would be forfeited and 'applied to the expenses of the institution'. However, there were times when this rule could be overlooked, depending on the patient's circumstances.

The next committee meeting was held on 13th August 1813, when a sub-committee recommended a house in Back Street (now Clare St) as suitable premises. The rent was £35 annually with an additional £5 for a portion of the garden. It was already occupied by a tenant, who agreed to surrender his lease to the owner Mr William Evans, for a sum of £35, so as to make the property available for immediate possession. Another sub-committee, consisting of all the medical officers, was appointed to 'arrange the fitting up of the Apothecary's Shop' which was to be situated in the left hand room on the ground floor. Another sub-committee was responsible for ordering and purchasing 12 cast iron bedsteads, bedding, furniture, kitchen equipment and 'to procure a proper woman to reside in the house as a nurse'.

There was no formal training for 'nurses' at this time – they were more like domestic servants. Nurse training was to come much later in the 19th century, encouraged by Florence Nightingale and others. The Matron of a hospital was usually a respectable woman, often a widow from the town, whose role was that of housekeeper. The 'nurses' in these institutions were drawn from the poorer working classes. At Bridgwater, Mrs Nancy Burrows was engaged as Matron at a salary of 12 guineas annually. The small institution was opened to patients on Sunday morning, 6th October 1813, just over 3 months from the date of the first meeting at the Grand Jury Room – something of a record, even at that time!

One can only surmise that Jonathan must have been delighted with such quick progress and would have been keen to make a success of the establishment. This would certainly require a great deal of hard work and perseverance.

It is noteworthy that success in any one institution might impact on other provision. For example, it was noted at the Wiveliscombe Infirmary that there was a drop in income in 1816 and this was thought to be due to the establishment of the new infirmaries in Taunton and Bridgwater. However, an encouraging comment from the Wiveliscombe committee in that year remarked that they should not regard these other infirmaries with jealousy but 'contemplate them with exaltation and pride' and the Governors should 'congratulate themselves in influencing them.'

Chapter 8

Ups and Downs

County hospitals require large sums for their formation, and considerable funds for their annual support; but the necessary means for establishing and maintaining small local institutions, are within the reach of most towns and populous villages. Jonathan Toogood

Jonathan was still a young man when the small institution was opened in Back Street in October 1813. At age 29 he must have felt very pleased with his efforts so far and was probably filled with energy and idealism. He would have been very much aware that he needed to work hard in his private practice, which after seven years he was still trying to establish. He would, of course, receive no payment for any duties undertaken at the small dispensary (note: at this point in time it was not yet referred to as Bridgwater Infirmary). He was already the father of three young boys, aged 5, 4 and 2 and his wife Ann was expecting again. World events would no doubt have been a matter of concern to his family. England after all was still in the throes of the Napoleonic Wars. He would have kept up to date by reading the London newspapers obtained from the general store in the Cornhill. Ironically the spire of St Mary's Church in Bridgwater was hit by lightning in 1813 and some viewed this as a bad omen.

On 20th October 1813 a further meeting took place to discuss rules for the election of medical staff. The physicians were to have studied and obtained degrees from a British University, and to present a written testimonial. The surgeons were to be members of the Royal College of Surgeons of London. Election was by majority vote at a general meeting, with the President having the casting vote, notice having been given in one of the Taunton newspapers one month preceding the meeting. Two physicians and three surgeons were to be elected and they were to reside within a mile's radius of the town. A rota was set up for Sunday morning admissions, the patient remaining under the care of the medical officer who had arranged the admission. Meetings were to take place at 10 o'clock on the first Monday of every month, when the apothecary shop was inspected and accounts audited. Rules for in-patients were also discussed at this meeting – some have already been alluded to in the previous chapter. However, the one rule that today would raise a few eyebrows was: 'That convalescent patients, and such as are capable, do, at the request of the matron, assist in cleaning the wards and attend to the other patients'.

Over the next four years 116 in-patients were admitted and 358 outpatients were treated. Unfortunately the institution's financial position became increasingly troubled and by 1st September 1817 the arrears due from subscribers were £621 13s 0d. Subscriptions in 1813 were £277 4s

0d, but these steadily decreased and were only £18 18s 0d in the year 1817. This was becoming an unsustainable situation and action was required.

Dr Marshall Hall, one of the physicians at the time, and Jonathan Toogood took it upon themselves to set out the financial difficulties of the institution and an urgent appeal was sent out to subscribers and donors for funds. At the sixth anniversary meeting of the management committee held on 15th January 1820, the then President, Joseph Jeffery, drafted a letter to be sent to landholders in the neighbourhood, asking for donations as the dispensary was unable to continue on the present subscriptions. At that same meeting, Mr Chubb stood down as Treasurer and Secretary, and Mr Charles Trevor was elected in his place. Sir Alexander Hood was appointed President.

Looking back on this financial crisis, the Infirmary report of 1840 quotes directly from a letter written by John Bowen (a subscriber of the institution) to Joseph Ruscombe Poole Esq, a gentleman of the town, recalling how at the end of 1819 'the infirmary appears to have been insolvent, and that nothing short of the most vigorous measures could have preserved it from destruction'. Bowen praised Sir Alexander Hood and Mr Charles Trevor for their joint efforts in increasing funds, and pointed out that they were 'powerfully aided by the untiring zeal of Mr Toogood'.

By 1820 the small house in Back Street had become insufficient to serve the needs of the community. In *A Bridgwater Diary 1800-1967* by Philip Squibbs, he comments that 1820 appeared to be a time of 'distress' in the town, maybe due to a hard winter, when the local masons gave a sum of money to alleviate 'the hardships of the poor.' This 'distress' would certainly have had an effect on the general health of the town. A house and garden in Salmon Lane (later known as Salmon Parade), along the east side of the river Parrett, previously owned by the late Mr W.H. Holloway, was offered by his executors for the sum of £700. After energetic and successful fund-raising (combined with the negotiation of a mortgage of £400), the property was bought and became formally known as The Bridgwater Infirmary. Subscriptions had risen to £165 17s 6d in the year 1820 and £473 14s 5d had been received in donations. About £60 was required to purchase new fixtures and fittings, and compensation had to be paid to Mr Evans for surrendering the lease of the old premises in Back Street. Jonathan offered to supply the institution with medicines and dispense the same for one year for £70, that being £10 less than any other tender.

An annual sermon (an event started in 1820) was given at St Mary's Church in aid of funds for the infirmary and it was noted in the infirmary minutes that on 9th November 1821 the Right Revd Lord Bishop of Gloucester gave an excellent sermon. These sermons brought in much needed funds and continued through the century. Preachers came from surrounding towns and villages, and the Bishop of Bath and Wells himself made several appearances. Jonathan's eldest son, Jonathan James Toogood, Vicar at North Petherton in the 1830s, preached the sermon in 1837 when £30 was collected.

In time, money was also raised at events such as an annual dinner and local concerts – the gentlemen of the Bridgwater Glee Club gave the infirmary very generous donations. Benefactors included several members of Jonathan's family – in 1823 Mrs Susannah Toogood from Sherborne, Jonathan's aunt by marriage to Charles Toogood, presented the institution with a donation of £100 which, with £25 from Jonathan himself, was to be used for the purpose of creating a sinking fund for paying off the £400 mortgage. Other members of the Toogood family also donated to the cause, as did those of his wife Ann. Ann's brother Captain Joseph Giles, who was manager of Stuckey's Bank in Wells, was a subscriber along with his wife Maria, and had been part of the management committee back in 1817. In fact Stuckey's Banking Company in Bridgwater donated £25. Ann's nephew, John Allen Giles became a subscriber and among the many subscribers in the early days is the name Hill Dawe, Jonathan's old 'master'.

Yet another way of raising money was to have future medical pupils pay a fee of 10 guineas for their training, or alternatively 2 guineas annually. In 1829 it was proposed that Jonathan take on an apprentice, who would be attached to the Infirmary. It had been agreed that a certificate of attendance should not be awarded to any pupil who had not strictly conformed to the rules.

τ

Bridgwater Infirmary gradually came of age – new wards were added in time, more equipment purchased and Jonathan presented the infirmary with an 'impressive fracture bed' in 1833. This was probably the type designed by Mr Earle, illustrated in *The Lancet* in 1824, and was intended for convalescing patients.

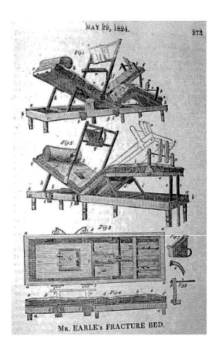

Fig. 15 Mr Earle's Fracture Bed

In 1827 (according to Squibbs) there was a 'prevalence of ague' in Bridgwater and its neighbourhood; the number of cases was 'astonishingly great" and there was a great deal of typhus fever during the same period, which no doubt would have put an extra strain on the infirmary. For decades to come, regular reports in the local newspaper kept the public informed not only about the infirmary's workload but also its finances. The extract below refers to medical cases only, without reference to surgical cases, emergencies, out-patients etc.

BRIDGWATER INFIRMARY.
Medical Cases of the above Institution for the last six months.

Uterine and Fits	1	In the House.
Consumption	1	Died.
Apoplexy	1	Died.
Affection of the Nerves (Neuralgia)	4	Three cured, one incurable, —discharged.
Ulceration of the Bowels	1	Incurable,—discharged.
Dropsy	2	Cured.
Tic Douloureux	1	Cured.
Stricture of the Bowels	1	Incurable,—discharged.
Inflammation of the Peritoneum	1	Cured.
Melancholy..........	1	Made surgeons patient.
Inflammation of the Bladder	1	Much relieved, made out-patient.
Cutaneous	1	Cured.
Affection of the Lumbar Nerves	1	Much relieved, discharged by her own request.
Scurvy..............	1	Discharged at his own request.
Fever	3	One died—two in the house.
Diarrhœa............	1	In the house.
Dyspepsia	2	Cured.
St. Vitus's Dance	1	Much relieved, discharged. to make room.
Rheumatism	1	Cured.

Signed, W. R. CUBITT, M.D.
January 24th, 1831.

Fig.16 Six monthly report from *Bridgwater & Somersetshire Herald* Jan 1831

The total number of patients attending the infirmary from 1st September 1838 to 1st September 1839 was 1,627. Records regarding accidents showed that in the same year 41 people were admitted as in-patients and 214 seen as out-patients. A large number of children (426) were vaccinated against smallpox. Only five years before in 1833, 40 people had died from smallpox in the town.

Housekeeping expenses for that period are listed below. Candles were still an essential commodity to light the establishment, and wood and coal were used for heating the wards and for cooking.

Meat -	£62– 6s – 6d
Bread & flour -	£61– 7s – 4d
Bacon, cheese, soap & candles -	£22–13s – 5 1/2d
Groceries -	£40–14s – 7 1/2d
Butter, eggs, milk -	£37– 6s– 9 1/2d
Coals, turf & wood -	£22–15s – 7 1/2d
Beer, cider, wine & spirits -	£22–15s – 2d
Washing, assistance, nurses, house expenses	£21– 8s – 1d
Servant's wages -	£13– 6s – 0d
Potatoes & other vegetables -	£ 9– 0s – 2d
Matron's salary -	£14–14s – 0d
Total:	£328 – 4s – 9d

Other expenses that year –
Building 2 new wards & various repairs -	£121– 7s–11d
Furniture -	£ 34– 4s– 4d
Sundries -	£ 9– 3s – 9d
Printing & Stationery -	£ 17–16s – 8d
Insurance & Gratuity -	£ 5–17s – 6d
Medicines -	£ 82–16s – 8d
House Apothecary's salary -	£ 50– 0s – 0d
Subscriptions for 1838 not received -	£ 6–16s – 6d
Balance in the hands of R. Woodland, treasurer	£112–11s – 9d
Grand Total:	£768–19s -10d

This was an enormous amount of money to have to raise in order to run the infirmary, equivalent to £62,440 today (*using the RPI from 1838-2015*). It was a tribute to the efforts of the management committee, who worked tirelessly to bring in subscriptions and find donors and benefactors.

There were always problems with retaining a House Apothecary and many came and went over the years. They did receive a salary (£50 as shown above) and they were actually the only medical staff to be paid. However, they had a full-time workload with the following duties:– preparing and dispensing medicines as directed; daily bleedings, scarifying and cupping; blistering and applying dressings; care of all surgical instruments.

In 1830 there was disapproval of the conduct of the matron Mrs Burrows, who had been in post since the foundation of the institution. It is unclear exactly what she had done to warrant this, but it led to her dismissal and a Mrs Alexander was appointed Matron in her place. Not everyone approved of the way the infirmary was run. In 1832 there was a letter from the Revd Robert Davis of Cannington, responding to a request for him to advocate the charity in his church. This he declined to do, unless the day for seeing patients was changed from a Sunday, the Lord's Day, to a weekday – only then would he consider preaching the annual sermon.

In 1849 a serious epidemic of cholera reached the town and it was agreed to relax the rule that disallowed patients with diarrhoea to be admitted, which resulted in a total of 1,000 people receiving assistance. This was in sharp contrast to the Taunton and Somerset Hospital that was unable to admit sufferers due to lack of facilities but they did treat patients without recommendations in their out-patient department. Sadly over 200 people died in Bridgwater (according to Squibbs), 88 of these poor souls are commemorated by a memorial stone in the graveyard at St John Eastover.

τ

The ups and downs continued of course, as in all establishments, but the infirmary did survive and prosper. In the 1850s Jonathan wrote a piece about public institutions for the relief of the sick, which was later published in the *British Medical Journal* in 1863. In this he again praises small dispensaries, especially the Wiveliscombe Infirmary, commenting that it 'dispensed more good, than any other charity with which I am acquainted on a similar scale'. From this article you certainly get a feeling for the passion he had for his work and for his belief in the medical profession, as exemplified in the quote below:

'The establishment of an hospital confers great benefits in a locality on all classes. It holds out an inducement to well educated men to settle in the neighbourhood; for, where hospitals exist, skilful medical men are always found. It is a great advantage also to students, who will find themselves much further advanced at the expiration of their pupilage, than those who have not enjoyed such opportunities.'

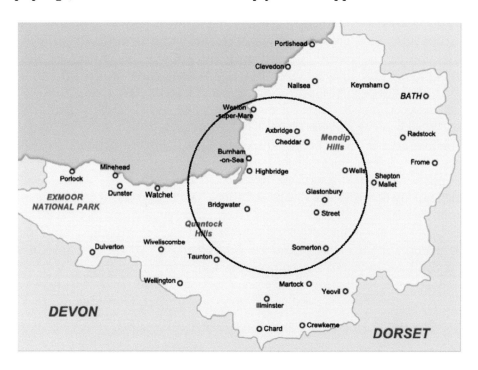

Fig.17 Map showing catchment area for
Bridgwater Infirmary by 1830s

Bath	1742
Wiviliscombe	1804
Taunton	1812
Bridgwater	1813
Chard	1842
Wells County Asylum	1848
Dunster & Minehead	1867
Crewkerne	1867
Yeovil	1872

Table 1 Foundation dates for Somerset Hospitals and Infirmaries

Chapter 9

Professional Colleagues

The great aim and object of medical science is to cure disease, and I, for one, am always glad to avail myself of the experience of practical men, in obscure and difficult cases, however lightly they may be esteemed by some
Jonathan Toogood

In an age before technology, handwritten letters were the only form of communication with distant colleagues, so when Jonathan sought advice from his medical brethren concerning one of his patients, he would put pen to paper. Sadly only a few of these letters have survived but they do give us an insight into the medical network in the 19th century.

The mail would have been delivered to the town of Bridgwater by mail coaches, which were painted black with maroon doors and red wheels. The doors displayed the Royal Coat of Arms and the mail guards were dressed in scarlet coats with blue lapels and gold trim, and they would sound a special horn to announce their arrival. The postmaster would collect the sack of mail and hand over the outgoing post. By the 1840s the railways had replaced these coaches and by then there was a main post office in St. Mary Street. There were three deliveries a day – letters cost a penny to send (the Penny Post) and could be posted up to 10 o'clock in the evening to catch the first delivery in London the following morning.

Photo from an old print by Mr. W. H. Kitch
THE WESTERN MAIL COACH

Fig.18 Bridgwater mail coach

In 1810 Jonathan wrote to Dr Willan in London asking advice about a patient (Mr H) who was suffering from psoriasis, a skin condition causing scaly patches, which even today can prove difficult to treat. Dr Robert

Willan (1757–1812) studied medicine in Edinburgh but settled in London and was appointed physician to the new Carey Street Public Dispensary where he remained for 21 years. He is remembered for his work on classification of skin diseases and today is considered to be the 'Father of Dermatology'.

Plate 22 Robert Willan
(1757-1812)
Wellcome Library

There are two letters in reply to Jonathan's regarding the patient (Mr H) and these are signed off by Dr Willan "believe me yours truly", the second of which reads as follows:

September 5th 1810

I would recommend you give Mr H-----, at the present season, the tincture of cobalt, introduced by the late Dr. De Valangin, and found to be much more safe and more efficacious than Fowler's Solution, which can be obtained from the Apothecaries Hall, under the title "Solvens Minerale Muriaticum.' The dose would be from eight to twenty drops three times a-day, in 11/2oz. Decoct. Cinchon, vel Ulmi, between meals, using two or three drops less, if any dose mentioned occasion nausea.

Two aspects of this letter are of interest – the first is the use of Latin, the preferred language used by the physicians at that time and in which they would have been well versed; and the second is the mention of the Apothecaries' Hall. The Worshipful Society of Apothecaries of London split from the Company of Grocers and was granted a royal charter in 1617. They acquired a hall in the City of London from the Black Friars, who occupied a Dominican Priory at that time, and this was renamed the Apothecaries' Hall. It still stands today on the same site in the area of the City which became known as Blackfriars. The Society of Apothecaries formulated, produced and sold their medicines from 1672 until 1922 and the building houses a wonderful display of medicinal jars that were once used to store the various preparations. It is quite possible that Jonathan acquired the remedy suggested by Dr Willan from the Apothecaries Hall as he goes on to comment: 'The patient recovered perfectly'.

Jonathan also consulted with John Abernethy regarding medical matters (as illustrated in a previous chapter) and remained in contact with another old tutor, namely Dr John Clarke. In a letter dated 1815, Dr Clarke discusses treatments including the management of haemorrhage following delivery of the placenta. It is the beginning of this correspondence that sheds some light on Jonathan's character. Clarke states that he had wanted to call on Jonathan in Bridgwater on his way from Bath to Devonshire, but was required to take an alternative route and had 'missed the pleasure of seeing you'. He goes onto say: 'it gives the most sincere satisfaction to learn that you are going on so prosperously. I never had a doubt that it would be so because you were indefatigable in laying in a good store of information and I never knew that fail when combined with a good understanding'. It is unlikely that Jonathan did get to see his old teacher again as Dr Clarke died that year at the age of 54 and he is buried in the Parish Church at Tamworth, Staffordshire.

Another letter dated 4th October 1814 arrived from Henry Cline of Lincoln's Inn Fields. Henry Cline (1750-1827) was a surgeon at St Thomas's Hospital in London, who also lectured in anatomy and was one of the examiners at the Royal College of Surgeons. He was offering advice to Jonathan concerning treatment of a condition affecting the jawbone.

Plate 23 Henry Cline
(1750-1827)

Another of Jonathan's contacts was Sir Astley Cooper (1768-1841), who became one of the most famous surgeons of his era, eventually obtaining the role of Sergeant-Surgeon to the Royal family. As a young man, his career had not started well – he was vain, lazy and sought glamour and excitement. He commenced his medical training as an apprentice to his uncle, William Cooper at Guy's Hospital, but this was unsuccessful. He was lodging with Henry Cline at the time and it was he who recognised the potential in the young student and encouraged him to pursue his studies in anatomy and surgery. Cooper was eventually appointed surgeon to Guy's Hospital in 1800 and went on to become one of the most industrious and therefore richest surgeon of his time. His knowledge of anatomy was outstanding and led to innovative surgery. He employed body-snatchers to provide him with a constant supply of corpses for dissection and study, culminating in the publication of numerous anatomical works. His most famous student was the poet John Keats, who admired him greatly.

Plate 24 Sir Astley Cooper
(1768-1841)

In the 1820s and 30s Jonathan consulted with Sir Astley Cooper, who replies in a friendly manner with helpful advice regarding the patients' conditions. One case concerning a lost catheter has already been discussed in chapter 6; another, shown below, gives advice regarding treatment of some form of ulcerated lesion. One wonders just how many of these letters Sir Astley Cooper wrote to surgeons across the country in the course of his career.

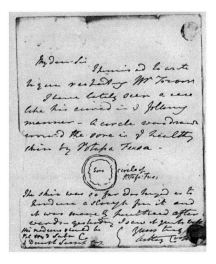

Fig.19 Copy of Sir Astley
Cooper's letter
dated 1823.
*King's College London
Archives*

On 3rd October 1831, *The Alfred*, which had replaced Bridgwater's first newspaper (The *Bridgwater and Somersetshire Herald*), reported the following:

'That most distinguished Surgeon, and accomplished Gentleman, Sir Astley Cooper, accompanied by his Lady, during a part of last week, favoured our highly respected townsman, Mr Toogood, with their company . . . [he] visited our Infirmary with Mr Toogood, and expressed his unqualified approbation of the most excellent Institution, the neatness, arrangement, and cleanliness of which he especially admired. He enquired minutely into the cases of many of the Patients . . . It is highly satisfactory to have the excellence of our Infirmary attested by such an experienced judge, as Sir Astley Cooper.'

This would have indeed been a great honour for Jonathan and would have given him an opportunity to discuss more surgical cases. He had previously 'furnished' Sir Astley with an example of a rare accident, namely the complete dislocation of the knee-joint, which Cooper subsequently included in his work *Treatise on Dislocations and Fractures of the Joints* published in 1822.

τ

Jonathan travelled a great number of miles to attend meetings and to visit colleagues across the country, for example to Scotland to visit his 'friend' Dr James Young Simpson in Edinburgh. Before the advent of the railways, he would have had to make the journeys by stage coach, which would have been long, uncomfortable and at times dangerous. One wonders whether he became accustomed to being a passenger on 'Swiftsure'.

In the summer of 1834 Jonathan visited Paris, although it is unclear whether this was his first visit to France, as he mentions having had a conversation with both Dupuytren and Roux about the knee-joint dislocation referred to above. Guillaume Dupuytren (1777-1835) became the chief surgeon at the Hôtel-Dieu in 1808 and was an excellent diagnostician and teacher, but he was ruthlessly ambitious, becoming one of the richest surgeons of his generation. He was not, however, a popular character and was known to his contemporaries as 'Le Brigand d'Hôtel-Dieu' and the 'Napoleon of Surgery'. The Hôtel-Dieu is the oldest hospital in Paris, dating back to AD 651; it overlooks the River Seine and stands next to Notre Dame.

Plate 25 Guillaume Dupuytren (1777-1835) *Wellcome Library*

Dupuytren is best remembered today for describing a condition in the palm of the hand causing the fingers to contract, known as Dupuytren's contracture. Philibert Roux (1780-1854) a military surgeon, succeeded Dupuytren as chief surgeon in 1835, and was an early pioneer in plastic surgery.

Plate 26 Philbert Roux
(1780-1854)
Wellcome Library

In 1834 Jonathan spent time at the Hospital of Venereal Diseases, later known as L'Hôpital du Midi, where he met with Philippe Ricord, the eminent venereologist of the 19th century. Ricord (1800-1889) was born in the USA and came to France at the age of 20, and joined Guillaume Dupuytren at the Hôtel-Dieu, where he didn't see eye to eye with his mentor and was dismissed. Ricord was a popular teacher and an excellent clinician; he was always very thorough in his examination of patients.

Plate 27 Philippe
Ricord (1800-89)
Wellcome Library

He promoted the vaginal speculum, an instrument dating back to Roman times but one that surgeons were reluctant to use. In the 1830s and '40s its use was hotly debated, as many practitioners were against its use on moral grounds. The French hospitals had a reputation for being less sensitive at using their patients as 'guinea pigs' for teaching purposes and therefore attracted many students. However, at a lecture given in 1843, published in the *Provincial Medical Journal*, Ricord explains in detail how the instrument is used and states:

> 'the medical man who rejects on this plea [that of indelicacy] examination with the speculum in uterine disease, and thereby wilfully deprives his patient of the vast advantage to be derived from ocular speculation, fails most signally in his duty, and offers an unwarrantable insult to the first of liberal professions in supposing its members capable of being actuated by unworthy motives at the sufferer's bedside.'

He goes on to say: 'The operation must be conducted throughout with the outmost decorum, and the slightest approach to levity should be altogether discarded.'

Jonathan watched Ricord using the speculum on many occasions during his visit and was impressed by the advantages of the device in helping to come to a clearer diagnosis and thus affording the patient more appropriate treatment. Once again he was content to buck the trend and employ an instrument that he considered helpful in managing disease. In 1841 he published an article in the *Provincial Medical & Surgical Journal* entitled 'On the Use of the Speculum', in which he remarks: 'It has been said that patients will not submit to its employment, but I have never yet met with a case in which it was necessary to use it, in which the most delicate woman objected to its use'. Maybe this says something about the trust he instilled in his patients. Today the speculum remains an integral part of a gynaecological examination and is essential for undertaking gynaecological procedures.

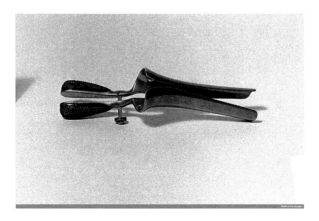

Fig.20 Speculum as used by Ricord *Wellcome Library*

There are two other gentlemen that Jonathan refers to in his writings and that are worthy of mention, illustrating the close links in the medical profession at that time. Firstly there was Dr John Blackall (1771-1860), who was physician to the Devon and Exeter Hospital and also practised in Totnes, where he was considered to be the physician of the district. He was a fine diagnostician and a kindly man – nothing was too much trouble.

Jonathan writes: 'I may be excused here, from acknowledging the pleasure and profit which a long intercourse with that distinguished physician has afforded me; and even now, I often refer to his letters with advantage'. Secondly, he refers to his 'friend' Dr Turner from Manchester. Thomas Turner (1793-1873), a contemporary of Jonathan's, was born in Truro, Cornwall and underwent his apprenticeship in Bristol, before completing his surgical training in London and Paris. He established a school of medicine in Manchester in 1825, which opened the way for future provincial medical schools, and was elected Surgeon to the Manchester Royal Infirmary in 1830. Jonathan visited Dr Turner in Manchester and a letter from the latter, addressed from Mosley Street, comments: 'It delights me very much to hear the prospect of my seeing you in Manchester on your way to Leeds.' In 1845 Turner writes that he is waiting for Jonathan to forward to him a paper discussing amputation for a case of traumatic gangrene of the arm but apologises for hurrying him, commenting rather amusingly: 'the "Printer's Devil" is treading on my heels'.

τ

It might be thought that Jonathan Toogood 'dropped names' in order to enhance his own career, but this is very unlikely. Articles in the journals at that time frequently referred to other members of the profession by name, along with their views, and so this was far from unusual. Today this takes the form of more formal references. Jonathan only names individuals in connection to the advice they gave him, either by letter or face to face, and it is very evident from his writing that he held many of these fellow professionals in great esteem and very much valued their contribution in order to serve his patients. What mattered most to him was providing the correct and best treatment to his fellow man.

Chapter 10

Toogood and the Law

The introduction of the new poor law has dealt a heavy blow and great discouragement against the medical profession Jonathan Toogood

With his work in the Infirmary, a busy private practice and a growing family, not to mention his attendance at meetings and correspondence with his medical friends and colleagues, you would be forgiven in thinking that Jonathan had enough to occupy his mind, let alone his time. Not so! There were many issues of the day that concerned him and his medical brethren; these were affecting society adversely and he was eager to enter into the debates in order to effect change. He would have been well aware of the small part his own father played in the campaign for the abolition of the Slave Trade and consequently was not afraid to air his views, even if at times these proved unpopular. This and the next two chapters take a look at some of his most strongly held views.

τ

From the outset, Jonathan was an opponent of the new *Poor Law Amendment Act* of 1834. This replaced a system of outdoor relief, which had existed for the poor since 1601. Under the old act Overseers of the Poor were responsible in each parish for providing care for anyone who fell upon hard times through unemployment, disability or illness. The poor could apply for aid, remaining in their own homes until their situation improved. In other words, relief was brought to the poor man's door. The magistrates were to ensure that the overseers fulfilled their duties, giving legal protection to those in need.

The 'old system', despite several amendments over the years, was proving unworkable in an increasingly complex society and had simply become too expensive. In 1832 Parliament set up a Royal Commission to look into ways of reducing the costs and stop abuses of the system, the latter were said to be particularly common in the South of England in agricultural areas. All this sounds familiar – in the 21st century we are still grappling with the same problems! In a nutshell the Commission recommended the following:– that outdoor relief should end; that parishes should be grouped together into Unions, the latter overseen by a Board of Guardians; and that relief should mainly be given in workhouses, which were to be made so undesirable that no-one would wish to go there voluntarily.

Prior to the new Act, there had always been some workhouses as part of the landscape but these were mostly used for the elderly, infirm and children. In the original Bridgwater Workhouse (est 1693), situated in Old Taunton Road, the occupants had been reasonably treated and were allowed little indulgences such as beer and tobacco.

Plate 28 The Old Bridgwater Workhouse designed to accommodate 86 inmates

With the passing of the Act in 1834, the existing workhouses in the country became inadequate for the needs of the poor and conditions became appalling with overcrowding and disease. This set in motion the building of new workhouses – Bridgwater Union Workhouse was established in 1837 in Northgate for 300 inmates. It was designed to accommodate the needs of 40 parishes, 39 of which were agricultural.

Plate 29 Bridgwater Union Workhouse built 1837; it became an NHS hospital in 1948 and was later known as Blake Hospital

Jonathan deplored the Poor Law Amendment Act, referring to it as 'that hard-hearted law'. He believed it to be detrimental to the medical profession that served the poor and made his feelings known in an article entitled *Parochial Medical Relief* printed in the *Provincial Medical & Surgical Journal* in July 1843. After 40 years of medical practice, Jonathan was well aware of the needs of his poor patients and in the article he reported that he had discussed the matter with the Assistant Commissioner of the Bridgwater Union at the time it was being set up. He knew every inch of the locality and the difficulties in reaching some of these rural settings, and considered the new medical districts too large for the surgeons to work effectively. The Commissioner, 'an entire stranger to the neighbourhood', paid no heed to Jonathan's advice and appointed seven surgeons to undertake the care of forty parishes – work that had previously been undertaken by seventeen practitioners.

The Poor Law Commission, based in Somerset House in London, enforced a uniform and centralised pattern of administration. They appointed a team of Assistant Commissioners, who set up the election of the local Boards of Guardians and provided the link between those guardians and the Poor Law Commission. In 1835 Robert Weale, a solicitor from Sussex was appointed Assistant Commissioner for Gloucestershire, Worcestershire and Somerset, creating 37 Unions of which 17 were in Somerset.

The Bridgwater Union, made up of the forty parishes, was divided into seven medical districts, each the responsibility of one medical officer, as described by Jonathan. The duties of these medical officers were many – they were either contracted to 6 or 8 rural parishes over a vast area (a scattered population with long distances between them); or they were appointed to the Union Workhouse itself with 300-400 inmates, of which there might be as many as 50-60 sick people at any one time. In all these cases they were required to supply the appropriate medicines and surgical appliances; attend women in labour; act as vaccinator; register births, deaths and marriages (the Registration Act was passed in 1836); and they were expected to undertake all this work for a 'pittance'. Many were also trying to attend to their private practices – a midwifery patient, for example, could well tie up the practitioner for 24-36 hours, sometimes longer – and there were always other urgent cases that needed attention.

Jonathan believed it would be very difficult for these medical officers to undertake the work satisfactorily and, as a consequence, the poor would be neglected. He saw many women die in labour due to lack of proper assistance and was convinced that such fatalities had increased amongst the poor since the introduction of the new Act. He cites an example of 'a poor, but most industrious and respectable woman', who had previously required at least one parish surgeon to attend her in her labours but who was refused assistance by the board of guardians in a subsequent confinement despite her husband's appeals. The woman died due to haemorrhage, leaving five children.

Jonathan contrasted parochial medical relief to that of the Voluntary Hospitals, where the medical staff were elected by merit and their posts were associated with dignity. In the Infirmary there were as many as three medical officers and often an 'in house' resident surgeon as well. The Parish Medical Officers, on the other hand, were 'obtained by pecuniary competition', which, he believed, degraded the holder. Jonathan was likewise critical of the medical men who took advantage of the system, advertising their services to families to attend them in their own homes and to supply medicines at four to five shillings a week, under-cutting the commissioners. He thought this brought shame to the medical profession and commented that the poor 'are often reduced to the greatest destitution from having pawned every thing they can part with to satisfy these rapacious men, who, like true Shylocks, insist on being paid beforehand; and these poor creatures declare that they have been driven to such a dreadful alternative by having the fear of the union house before their eyes'.

Jonathan advocated a reduction in the size of the districts, thus subdividing the workload, upholding the honour of the medical profession and dissuading practitioners from pandering to the poor law commissioners: 'Until such desirable objects are obtained, the poor must continue to suffer.'

Abraham King, a young surgeon with only two years experience, was appointed to the Union Workhouse and the Borough of Bridgwater in May 1836 and was one of these young men hoping to build up a private practice in the area as well. Along with other medical officers, he complained that they were underpaid. The Provincial Medical Association took up their cause, threatening to boycott anyone who accepted employment by the board. Unfortunately this fate befell John Rodney Ward, who had replaced Abraham King and who for two years underwent harassment until finally he was found guilty of negligence at the Assize Court in Wells. He only held the Licentiate from the Society of Apothecaries and had no formal qualification in surgery. His case was used to advance the argument for the union medical officers to hold both qualifications.

The obsession with saving money led the Assistant Poor Law Commissioner in Bridgwater to provide a very inadequate daily diet to the inmates of the Workhouse and to remove those small indulgences given, such as beer. Worst of all, he disallowed the use of the pall and tolling of the bell at funerals. This disrespect for the dead was particularly painful to the poor in Victorian times and fortunately it was rescinded.

τ

Another aspect of the law that disturbed Jonathan, and others, was that of the role of coroners. There were a number of reports in the medical press concerning the inadequacies of coroner's courts in the 1840s and Jonathan's articles were some of the most outspoken, describing the inquests held by coroners as 'often solemn farces and mere mockeries of justice'.

The role of the coroner dates back to 1194 and was initially created to investigate any aspect of medieval life that may potentially benefit the crown. For example, those found guilty of *Felo de se* or 'self murder' (in today's terms suicide) would forfeit all their goods and chattels to the crown. Besides this, they were denied burial in consecrated ground – a very serious verdict for the grieving families. It became more and more apparent that inquests were not conducted in the best interest of the person who had died and in many instances the court's costs became the overriding priority. Another concern at that time was that due to the easy availability of poisons, especially arsenic, it was feared that many homicides went undetected. This will be addressed in more depth in the next chapter.

Jonathan was unashamedly critical of coroners and wrote: 'this important office is too often held by low ignorant men, who are totally unfitted for it by their education or acquirements and who seek it to supply the deficiency of income, which the failure of their occupation, either from want of ability or industry, has occasioned'. Harsh words and rather reminiscent of those of his grandfather John Toogood, who was less than flattering about members of staff at Sherborne School when he was a governor there.

Jonathan believed strongly that the role of the coroner was vitally important: 'It concerns the morals, the lives and the liberties of the community'. He called for the law to be amended and he was not alone. Many reports in the 1840s described tragic events which were inadequately investigated and resulted in dismissive verdicts such as 'Died by the visitation of God' or *Felo de se*. One case was that of Mr William Trevor, a surgeon in the town of Dulverton, Devon, writing in the *Provincial Medical and Surgical Journal* (9th July 1845) regarding a young servant woman. She had taken poison, believing that she was pregnant by a man whom she subsequently saw walking out with another woman. In her final four days of suffering, she was attended by Mr Trevor and confided in him about the pregnancy, confessing that she had taken poison. Very few witnesses were called to the inquest and Mr Trevor was not allowed to give evidence – 'Because if he was examined, he would be entitled to a fee of one guinea!' In consequence he was unable to speak of her state of mind, the verdict was *Felo de se* and she was buried without funeral rites. William Trevor commented: 'those who know anything of the feelings of the labouring classes, will be able to estimate the additional agony thus inflicted upon the wounded hearts of the distressed parents'. A reporter at the inquest described how Mr Trevor had pleaded with the coroner that no evidence had been given concerning her state of mind but the coroner replied 'Leave the room sir, I will not have these interruptions' and forbade him from publishing the account in the newspapers. Mr Trevor, however, replied that 'I most certainly shall do', at which point the coroner demanded that he be turned out of the courtroom. Jonathan commented on this case two weeks later, pointing out the necessity of post-mortem examinations and on the failure to call important witnesses, stating 'the purse of the public is treated with more respect than their lives.'

There were several other reports written by surgeons from around the country, agreeing with Mr Toogood. They cited examples of inquests where the request for a post-mortem and/or evidence from medical witnesses were refused by the coroner. Mr Stead, a surgeon from Harrogate, recalled how 'the magistrates at Pontefract sessions had complained of the enormous amount of money expended in fees to medical witnesses'. He described the case of an elderly man who had cut his throat. Mr Stead had been called to attend the victim and consequently had expected to be summoned as a medical witness, in order to give evidence regarding the old chap's state of mind. The jury also requested his testimony but the coroner said: 'they might ask him any question, but he could not allow him a fee' – as a result the surgeon left the room! Other articles at this time told of similar cases where post-mortems were refused and fees declined. It is important to note that there were no pathologists to perform the autopsies, as we would expect today, but instead the local surgeon would undertake the examination. Jonathan performed many post-mortems during the course of his career.

Probably the best-known and most outspoken campaigner for reform of coroners' inquests was Thomas Wakley (1795-1862). Wakley was born in Membury, Devon and was educated at Chard and Taunton grammar schools, before being apprenticed at first to Thomas Incledon, an apothecary in Taunton. He eventually completed his surgical training at the United Hospitals of St Thomas's and Guy's where Sir Astley Cooper was surgeon. Wakley held very radical views and in 1823 started the medical journal *The Lancet*, along with journalist William Cobbett, James Wardrop and a libel lawyer. At first the journal set about exposing medical corruption, especially attacking the Royal College of Surgeons. Wakley remained editor until his death in 1862. He became a radical Member of Parliament in 1835 for the constituency of Finsbury, and was made coroner for West Middlesex in 1839 – the first medically qualified coroner in London. He called for reform in many aspects of public medicine – a humane supply of corpses for dissection; a comprehensive register of medical practitioners; and the raising of standards of coroners' inquests (arguing that coroners should be medically trained), to name but three.

Plate 30 Thomas Wakley
(1795-1862)
Wellcome Library

Jonathan refers to Wakley's views when discussing his own observations of inquiries into the cause of death. He states that inquests 'are too frequently conducted in a careless and slovenly manner as to become a mere matter of fact; the verdicts are often returned from partial and imperfect evidence, and sometimes without evidence at all'. He goes on to say: 'In this part of the country the evidence of a medical man is generally dispensed with, and post-mortem examination is a matter of very rare occurrence'. From examples already given, it is apparent that this was a concern countrywide. He regrets that when he was Mayor of Bridgwater in 1823 and sat in the Bridgwater Quarter Sessions in the Guildhall, he did not fully comprehend the extent of the coroner's power. He remembers a case of a man who was involved in a fight and died a few hours later. At the inquest Jonathan refused to give evidence without making an examination first, which was granted reluctantly. At post-mortem he discovered that a large artery had ruptured and that there was a considerable quantity of blood in the brain. He explained this to the coroner and the jury but was astonished when the verdict was returned as 'accidental death'.

Jonathan's separate concerns about the new Poor Law and about the performance of coroners were actually brought together in the scandal of the Bridgwater Union Workhouse in the 1830s. He observed that if Wakley had been the coroner in the (Bridgwater) district 'during that awful period when 40 per cent of the poor perished in the Bridgwater Union, inquest upon inquest would have been held and his labours would have occupied a year in the inquiry; but those victims were silently passed to their graves – no judicial inquiry of any kind was instituted'.

By 1836 the conditions in the old Bridgwater workhouse had become utterly appalling. The new Bridgwater Union administration had begun in May 1836, so paupers from all 40 parishes could now be sent to the old workhouse, pending the construction of the new larger workhouse building (which would not open until 1837). The old house was desperately overcrowded with 3 adults or 6 children to one bed, many suffering from measles or other infectious conditions. Diarrhoea was rampant and many inmates were so weakened that they lay in their own excrement. The medical officer at the time, Abraham King, called for a change in diet and was convinced that the oatmeal the children were given in place of milk was partly responsible for the continued diarrhoea. His pleas fell on deaf ears and it was made very plain to him that the diet was of no concern of his, that he should attend the sick and that only. At one time even the medical officer, the master and his family were all affected and it was becoming impossible to engage help in the form of nurses and servants.

An extract from the surgeon's book listed the inmates and their illnesses, as shown in the table below.

Number	Medical Condition	Age
6	Measles complicated by diarrhoea	4 & under
2	Inflammation of the lungs complicated by diarrhoea	1, 2 years
1	Tubercles on lungs complicated by diarrhoea	2 years
1	Ulcer in the bowels complicated by diarrhoea	2 years
3	Marasmus (malnutrition) with diarrhoea	6mths - 4
1	Natural decay complicated by diarrhoea	78
1	Consumption complicated by diarrhoea	23
1	Rupture of blood vessel complicated by diarrhoea	44
10	Diarrhoea	All ages
TOTAL 26		

Table 2 Illnesses recorded in one week (1837) at the old Bridgwater Workhouse
Somerset Heritage Centre

This was not a temporary 'blip' with infections continuing at a high level over at least a two year period – even in the new building (that housed over 300 inmates) 111 cases of disease were recorded on the day of January 16th 1839. Members of the visiting committee (who reported to the Board of Guardians) stated that the house had become so infectious that it would be dangerous to admit any more people, but they were ignored just as the surgeon had been. A total of 127 paupers were sent into the workhouse during this time. A member of the visiting committee in April 1837 found himself 'utterly unable to visit the wards', being totally overcome by the 'foetid stench' throughout the house which was so intolerable.

It was through the efforts of John Bowen (1785-1854), a wine merchant in the town and editor of *The Alfred* newspaper as well as anti-poor law campaigner, that the conditions of the Union workhouse were exposed. Bowen was an interesting character – he had grown up in Bridgwater, was self-educated and was at one time employed by the East India Company as an engineer building lighthouses. He reported that in the first 4 months of 1837, 30 inmates out of a total of 94 had died in the old workhouse. He contrasted such 'executions by meal and water' in just ONE workhouse with the prison system where only 17 executions took place in the whole of England and Wales in the year of 1836. The Poor Law Commission and the Assistant Commissioner were only concerned with saving money and no mentions were made of the poor living conditions at Bridgwater in a 'satisfactory' report of May 1837. Bowen did, however, manage to take the scandal of the Bridgwater Workhouse to a Parliamentary Select Committee, to be examined by 24 Peers in July 1838. Jonathan Toogood was called as a witness before this committee. It seems that the peers were far from sympathetic and, apart from the transfer of Assistant Commissioner Robert Weale to Staffordshire, very little changed. Many of the guardians on the board probably were well intentioned but were almost certainly out of their depth. As a final note, the Bridgwater Workhouse scandal grabbed public attention at the exact same time as the serialisation of Charles Dickens' *Oliver Twist* (Feb 1837-Apr 1839), which alluded to the poor diet of gruel among other observations.

τ

Jonathan's comments about the role of coroners found approval from many of the medical profession, as illustrated above. However, not everyone agreed and he was subjected to angry replies and abuse from some. He was, however, convinced that his views were correct and would not be distracted. In 1853 he wrote: 'It is high time that the whole body of the profession should be "up and stirring", to amend this antiquated law of coroner, and to protect themselves from incompetent coroners, illiterate juries, and malevolent rivals.' It took another 34 years for the Coroners Act to be repealed, with priority given to determining the circumstances and actual medical causes of sudden, violent and unnatural deaths for the benefit of the community as a whole.

Jonathan had his own brush with the law on more than one occasion. One of these episodes will be discussed in a later chapter, as it involved a homeopathic practitioner. Another case arose from a disagreement with a solicitor in Bridgwater by the name of George Henning Pain, who had written a letter stating that Toogood had 'uttered a falsehood respecting his character'. A copy of this letter denouncing Toogood as a coward was then distributed around the town in the form of handbills. The matter was settled in court and reported in *The Times* on 12th May 1832. Pain was found to be in the wrong and Toogood was awarded £100. No doubt this would have been a difficult and unpleasant time for Jonathan.

Chapter 11

The Great Arsenic Evil

The crime of secret poisoning has become so common in this country, that scarcely a week passes in which some instance is not brought before the public   Jonathan Toogood

The 1840s witnessed a frenzy of articles in both national and local newspapers with tales of poisoning with arsenic. There were a number of high profile cases that had slipped through unnoticed in the coroners' courts, the perpetrators free to repeat their crimes without detection. The medical press also picked up on these stories and were particularly concerned with the availability of the poison and the failure of the coroners to fully investigate suspicious deaths, often due to financial constraints, as discussed in the last chapter. However, not all of these cases were due to criminal action – in fact the vast majority were a result of accidental poisoning.

Arsenic could be bought anywhere and by anyone! As well as from druggists, it was available from grocers, chandlers, paint dealers, oilmen (selling lighting oil) and other traders. Half an ounce could be bought for a penny, the smallest amount that a druggist would offer for sale. 'A pennurth of arsenic for rat poison' became a popular catch phrase. A *Punch* cartoon in 1849 shows a little girl, hardly tall enough to look over the counter, asking the chemist for a pound and half of arsenic for the rats, to which he replies 'Certainly Ma'am'.

There were legitimate uses for arsenic, such as in many medicinal preparations. Some ointments contained arsenic and were used topically to treat skin diseases such as psoriasis. Probably the best known medicine at the time was the ubiquitous 'Fowler's Solution', prescribed by both regular and irregular practitioners for fever (especially 'ague') but also for many other complaints – a 'cure for all'. It was named after the Staffordshire physician Thomas Fowler, who in 1783 made up a solution of potassium arsenite. This was based on a traditional treatment known as 'The Tasteless Ague and Fever Drops', a remedy adopted by those living in the fens of East Anglia where malaria was common. It became so popular that in 1809 it was added to the list of approved medicines in the *London Pharmacopoeia* as 'liquor arsenicalis'. The solution had a touch of lavender added to give it a distinctive flavour.

Arsenic was used extensively in agriculture for steeping grain (as a fungicide), dipping sheep (4lb was required to dip 100 sheep), and for vermin control. Sold as a white powder, it could easily be confused with flour, sugar and cream of tartar. As farmers and shepherds often stored the poison in indoor cupboards in their cottages, accidental poisoning by food adulteration was a fairly common event, especially as it was odourless, tasteless and soluble in water. Even in the premises of druggists and grocers it could be mistaken for other compounds such as arrowroot and magnesia. In 1851 Dr James Tunstall of Bath, writing in the *Provincial Medical & Surgical Journal,* cited a case in Chew Magna, in North Somerset, where 14 people were nearly poisoned with arsenic sold to them by a baker's wife, who mistook it for carbonate of soda.

In the same journal in July 1845 Dr George Parker May of Maldon, Essex, reported the tragic case of a healthy child of twenty months who, when his mother's back was turned, retrieved from a closet that she had just unlocked, a small pot of paste which he consumed. On discovering what had happened, the mother quickly administered an emetic, which worked quickly, making the child vomit. Sadly this was in vain and the infant was dead within 8 hours. The paste was kept for destroying mice and contained a mixture of honey, flour and arsenic.

While on the subject of accidental poisoning, it should be pointed out that Victorians were also subjected to contamination with arsenic from numerous other sources. The green pigment Scheele's Green (copper arsenite) was found in wallpapers, curtains, dress fabrics and also turned up in confectionery. Taxidermy was popular in the 19th century, when arsenic was used as a preservative; stuffed birds and animals were very fashionable items in the Victorian home. Flypapers also contained arsenic. There were even adverts for arsenical facial products to enhance the appearance of the skin.

Fig.21 Example of arsenic advertisement

Arsenic was also used as an abortifacient but this would too often lead to the death of the pregnant woman. However, its use as a secret poison to commit murder was what excited the public and there were a number of trials that made headlines.

As there was no reliable form of contraception, Victorian families were large and children often became a burden financially to the poor. Many parents would pay into 'burial clubs' in order to avoid a pauper's funeral and some children were signed up to several of these clubs. These clubs were very affordable - a half-penny or penny a week - and on the death of the child the payout could be as much as £5 in some places, the average basic funeral only costing one to two pounds. If the child were enrolled with several clubs, a tidy sum could be made. It was rumoured that parents in the 19th century might sometimes dispose of their children for financial gain, arsenic being the chosen method. The symptoms from poisoning could easily be mistaken for a gastric complaint or other infection and would therefore go undetected.

It is therefore unsurprising that the medical profession rallied together to discuss ways to curb the sale of arsenic. Jonathan Toogood was at the forefront of this campaign. In 1845 following the trial and execution of Sarah Freeman for what became known as the Shapwick Murders, he suggested to the Bridgwater Town Council that they petition Parliament for legislation to restrict the sale of arsenic. Sarah Freeman from the village of Shapwick, near Bridgwater, had been arrested following the suspicious death of her brother Charles, a post-mortem confirming the presence of arsenic in his intestine and liver. Some 18 months earlier her husband Henry, her illegitimate son James Dimond and her mother Mary had all died. Her husband was a member of a burial club and she had received £20 as a result of his death. Suspicions were raised and the body of the child, James, was exhumed and chemical analysis was undertaken which proved the presence of arsenic. It was thought that she had in fact poisoned all four members of her family. In 1843 when the child died, the surgeon involved with the case offered to carry out a post-mortem but this was deemed unnecessary by the coroner due to the costs that would be incurred. Jonathan, writing to *The Times* (subsequently printed in *The Lancet* in May 1845), used this as an example of the failure of the coroner's court, remarking: 'This case affords another instance of the fearful effects of negligence in conducting a solemn judicial inquiry. If the parties whose business it was to investigate the cause of this poor child's death had faithfully and diligently performed their duty, the fact of poison having been taken would have been developed, and an immediate stop would probably have been put to these wholesale murders'. Sarah Freeman was hung on 23rd April 1845 at Wilton Gaol, in Taunton.

Bridgwater council responded to Jonathan's request and petitioned Parliament, at the same time addressing letters to Sir Robert Peel (Prime Minister) and Sir James Graham (Home Secretary), urging them to take the subject seriously. Jonathan later expressed his own concerns to Sir George Grey (the next Home Secretary) and likewise petitioned the House of Commons. Unfortunately all these pleas fell on deaf ears and no action was taken.

There had been earlier attempts at legislation dating back to 1819, when a bill was brought before the House of Commons. The proposal was that all containers of poisons should have a printed label bearing the word 'POISON' and it was further recommended that arsenic should have colour added. Contrary to what might be expected, the Society of Chemists and Druggists opposed the bill and it was withdrawn.

The science of forensic toxicology was born at the beginning of the 19th century in France with Mathieu Joseph Bonaventure Orfila (1787-1853) who attempted the classification of poisons. Robert Christison (1797-1882) attended Orfila's lectures in Paris and in 1822 became professor of medical jurisprudence in Edinburgh. William Herapath (1796-1868) from Bristol was the leading authority on toxicology in the West Country and was called upon to perform chemical tests to ascertain if a person had been poisoned. It was Herapath who analysed the samples from Charles Dimond's body in the Shapwick murders case.

Although tests for arsenic were available in the 18th century, none were very sensitive until the Marsh Test, which was devised in 1836 by James Marsh, a young chemist at the Royal Arsenal in Woolwich. The previous tests had relied on the precipitation of arsenic into a coloured compound but the results proved unreliable when other substances precipitated out at the same time, which would often occur when analyzing a sample of fluids taken from the stomach. The Marsh Test relied on the separation of arsenic as a volatile gaseous compound rather than a solid precipitate (*see Appendix 2 for an explanation as to how the test worked*). It remained one of the standard tests for arsenic until the 1970s.

τ

Jonathan was like a dog with a bone – once he got his teeth into something, he was determined to see it through until the end. On June 7th 1849 he wrote to Charles Hastings, President of the Council of the Provincial Medical and Surgical Association (PMSA), suggesting that the Council should present petitions to the two Houses of Parliament on behalf of its members, outlining measures to prevent the indiscriminate sale of poisons, especially arsenic. Jonathan's initial three proposals were as follows:

> 'That no druggist or shopkeeper should be allowed to sell arsenic, under a penalty, without a licence.'
> 'That no person should be able to purchase arsenic under any circumstances, unless accompanied by a witness.'
> 'That the vendor should be compelled to keep a book, in which he should make an entry of every such sale, to which the purchaser and his witness should affix his name and place of abode, and this should be attested by the vendor.'

As an illustration of how legislation could work, he described the strict rules that were in place in Austria at the time for the sale of medicines as well as the duties of the apothecaries there. At the next meeting of the South-Western branch of the PMSA in July, Jonathan, who was by now living in Torquay, formally recommended the above proposals on the sale of poisons. It was unanimously agreed that some 'legislative restriction' was necessary and that a Committee should be appointed at the next Anniversary Meeting of the PMSA to prepare a bill to this effect.

The 17th Anniversary Meeting was held at Worcester on 2nd August 1849. Jonathan was unable to attend this meeting but his paper on the subject of 'the practice of secret poisoning', was brought before the meeting by Dr Francis Sibson of London, a well-respected physician and teacher at St Mary's Hospital. Together Dr Tunstall of Bath, Mr Fuge of Plymouth, and Dr Sibson drafted a petition to be sent to Parliament incorporating Jonathan's ideas with the additional clause – 'That no person be allowed to sell small quantities of arsenic, unless combined with some material, the administration of which with food would be at once detected by taste.' They were committed to 'attack the great arsenic evil.'

During the course of the following year the committee, which had been modified to include Jonathan Toogood, Thomas Hodgkin MD FRS (a great friend of Dr Sibson) and Charles Hastings, worked tirelessly to put together a report under the title *To consider what restrictions should be placed upon the sale of arsenic and other poisons*. The committee had been able to obtain the co-operation of the Pharmaceutical Society of Great Britain, representing the druggists, which was an enormous step forward. Together they submitted their report and the following three resolutions went out to the Home Office in March 1850:

- That the retail sale of arsenic should be restricted to chemists and druggists and apothecaries.
- That arsenic should be sold to male adults or to their written order
- That the vendor should enter the sale in a book, with the date and object for which it was required, to which the applicant and a witness, one or other being known to the vendor, should sign their names, unless a written order be brought in a handwriting known to the vendor, which order should be pasted in the book.

Their report was read out by Dr Tunstall at the 18th Anniversary Meeting of the PMSA, held at Hull on 7th-8th August 1850. Tunstall had written to Lord Duncan, the MP for Bath, requesting that he bring the report to the attention of the Home Secretary, Sir George Grey. However, correspondence received only that day from that gentleman made it clear that he had 'no intention of bringing a bill to prohibit the sale of poisons this session'. The committee was determined to continue to agitate 'to accomplish our end' and it was agreed to petition Parliament again.

Unfortunately, Jonathan had again been unable to attend that PMSA meeting but Dr Sibson read out a letter received from him on this subject:

'My dear Dr Sibson, - You are aware of the cause which prevents me from meeting the members of the Association in Hull. I shall therefore be greatly obliged to you to express my regret at my inability to take part in the discussion on the indiscriminate sale of poisons, and my satisfaction that Government is taking up the question in the spirit of our resolutions, and of the petition I submitted, through you to the last meeting of the Association. I earnestly hope that the members will exert themselves individually to influence members of Parliament whom they may know, and impress them with the great importance of the subject. I have, as you know, devoted my earnest attention to this matter for some years past, and during the last year have received valuable assistance from the President, Dr Hodgkin, yourself, Dr Tunstall, and the Pharmaceutical Society, and I trust through our mutual co-operation, such resolutions will be adopted at the meeting, as will convince the Government of the absolute necessity of the speedy

legislative measure to check the crime of secret poisoning, which still prevails to a fearful extent.

As you so fully understand my views and feelings on this point, I must beg favour of your acting for me on this occasion.

I remain, dear Dr Sibson,

Very sincerely yours,

J. TOOGOOD

The reason for Jonathan's absence from these meetings was almost certainly due to ill health. Three years later he dedicated his book *Reminiscences of a Medical Life* to Dr Sibson, writing: 'I inscribe the following pages to you, in testimony of my esteem for your professional abilities, and private friendship; and in grateful acknowledgment of the skill, unremitting attention, and great kindness, with which you conducted me safely through a very severe and dangerous illness.' We shall never know from what physical illness Jonathan suffered, but it did not affect his mental capacity to continue fighting in the campaign for the legislation of the sale of arsenic.

The Sale of Arsenic Regulation Act was finally given its royal assent on 5th June 1851 and was passed into law. There were a number of changes to those proposed by the medical profession, possibly the most disappointing was that there was no restriction to the type of vendor – in other words anyone could still sell arsenic. However, the seller was bound to register the sale in a book, recording the date, name, address, and occupation of the purchaser; the quantity of arsenic sold; and the purpose for which it was required. The seller and purchaser both signed the book in the presence of a witness. In the original proposals, purchases were restricted to the male sex, which was almost certainly due to the number of high profile cases of poisoning perpetrated by women. However, women objected to this rule and this was changed to 'any person' over the age of 21. Quantities less than 10 pounds were required to be mixed with either soot or indigo in order to give the powder a colour and prevent accidental use. However, as was pointed out by a correspondent in *The Lancet* Dr Thomas Cattell, writing from Northamptonshire in December 1851, arsenic dissolves in water (unlike soot and indigo) and is thus quite easily separated out for criminal purposes. The Act did not, however, extend to the sale of arsenic when it formed a part of the ingredients of a medicine prescribed by a medical practitioner. There was to be a penalty of up to £20 for those abusing the Act.

This Act was only the start of restrictions to the sale of poisons. In 1868 The Pharmacy and Sale of Poisons Act tightened up the law by limiting sellers to pharmaceutical chemists and druggists, and all poisons sold had to be labelled 'POISON'. However, many deadly substances were still available as ingredients of other items, for example in weed killers. In 1908 there was actually a relaxation in the law, enabling ironmongers, storekeepers and other unqualified persons throughout the country to sell arsenic, provided that they obtained a licence from the local authority. It was another five decades before arsenical weedkillers were replaced by paraquat in 1962. Other poisons remained available and those familiar with the crime novels of Agatha Christie in the early 20th century will be aware of alternative options!

It is difficult to determine what the impact of the 1851 Act was on 'secret poisonings' and there is no record of Jonathan's views on the aftermath of the Act in which he had been so instrumental. At the 19th anniversary meeting of the PMSA in August that year, the following comment on the new bill was expressed: 'It will be admitted that this is an enactment in the right direction, and whatever may be the defects of the law, it cannot fail to produce good results'.

Chapter 12

Toogoodism

Quackery carefully conceals the number and extent of its victims
Jonathan Toogood

Quackery, as discussed earlier, had become a popular alternative to orthodox medicine in the 18th century. As well as the traditional view of the quack, standing on a soap-box in the market square waxing lyrical about his wonderful new cure for all ailments, there were other more exciting treatments based on the new phenomenon of electricity and magnetism. Benjamin Franklin (1706–1790), an American polymath, had been exploring electricity in the 1740s and spent a great deal of time in London, becoming a fellow of the Royal Society in 1756.

The idea that electricity could be the answer for curing all ills caused excitement amongst a number of entrepreneurs who took advantage of this science. One of these was James Graham (1745-1794) who was born and studied in Edinburgh. Although he failed to complete his medical training, this did not deter him from using the title of doctor. He visited the USA and became aware of Franklin's experiments, convincing himself and others that electrical treatments could be a universal cure. He returned to England, practising at first in Bath and then in London, where he opened his 'Temple of Health' in Pall Mall in 1779. Furnished lavishly with mirrors, pillars, crystals and statues, the rooms also contained impressive looking pieces of electrical apparatus. An invisible orchestra played soft music and the air was perfumed; within this atmosphere scantily clad women would pose among the statues and pillars. Graham also claimed that with the aid of electricity he could obtain ethereal extracts from drugs that could cure all ailments and he sold these as elixirs of life – for £1,000 patrons could receive a constant supply of these elixirs!

For just 2 guineas a patron could enter into this 'Temple' and wander around the sumptuous surroundings. There was even a throne room, known as the Grand Apollo Apartment, which contained an ornate throne, above which was suspended a crown which generated electrical charges. Graham also gave lectures with a strong sexual content, which were available for patrons to attend for an additional 6 guineas, and he became known as the sex therapist of his day. However, his most famous piece of apparatus was the luxurious 'Celestial Bed' with electrical charges crackling across the headboard that was guaranteed to treat sterility and impotence. Couples could hire the bed for the night for the exorbitant sum of £50! Although he attracted the rich and famous, his ventures eventually failed. He fell into debt and drifted into insanity.

A similar cult grew up in Austria at about the same time and subsequently became known as mesmerism, named after its founder, Franz Mesmer (1734-1815). Mesmer qualified in Vienna as a medical practitioner but soon held orthodox medicine in contempt, having come to believe in animal magnetism. This magnetism was influenced by the solar system – cosmology had been an important feature of ancient medical beliefs, so in some respects this was not a completely new idea. He used his 'magnetic therapy' to induce the patient to fall into a trance and used suggestion to relieve pain. This was still being debated in the 19th century, with the possibility of using mesmerism to control pain in surgery but anaesthesia eventually won that argument. Like Graham, Mesmer occupied fabulously furnished rooms, attracting the rich and the aristocracy – Marie Antoinette became one of his patrons. He is best remembered for his 'tub', a large round bath containing sulphuric acid from which iron bars protruded at intervals. *See Fig.22 below.* Clients were encouraged to sit round the tub, either holding hands or gripping the iron bars, when Mesmer would appear touching each person in different places on their body, sending them into a trance. Later experiments disproved the theory of animal magnetism but his ideas on the 'suggestibility' of patients persist today in modern hypnotherapy.

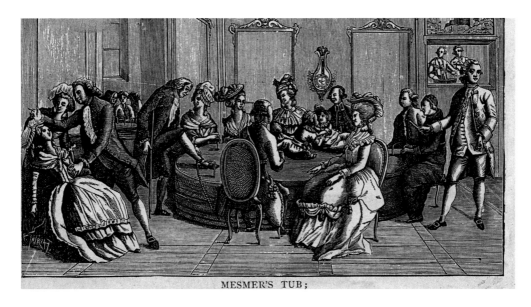

MESMER'S TUB;

Fig.22 Mesmer's tub *Wolloomo Library*

Another convert to the theory of using magnets as therapeutic agents was Elisha Perkins (1741-1799), who started life as a successful regular doctor in Connecticut, USA. Convinced, however, that metallic substances could cure all diseases, he invented two metal sticks (a mixture of metals, including gold and silver), which he sold at 5 guineas for the pair and were known as 'Perkin's tractors'. The sticks were drawn downwards over the affected part of the body for 20 minutes and effectively were sold as a 'do-it–yourself' form of treatment. His son brought the invention to England in 1797 and in 1804 founded the Perkinean Institute in Soho, London, which was supported initially by physicians, surgeons and the clergy. The metal sticks were not only used to treat human conditions but were also advertised for use on horses and dogs. Eventually, the tractors were dismissed as a 'cure for all' and were ridiculed by the cartoonists of the time.

Plate 31 James Gillray's cartoon, showing Elisha Perkins

Wellcome Library

By the beginning of the 19th century people had started to lose faith in some of these electrical methods and were eager to try other 'alternative treatments'. Many medical practitioners were also becoming disillusioned with orthodox medicine (especially its blood-letting and use of toxic compounds), believing these were doing more harm than good, which of course they were in many cases. We have already seen Jonathan's anxieties around the bleeding of patients and his cautious approach to some medications. Two new treatments, which began to attract attention with both the medical profession and the general public, were hydropathy and homeopathy.

Vincenz Priessnitz (1799-1851) was the son of an Austrian peasant farmer living in the district of Graefenburg, which was abundant in fresh springs. From a young age he believed that cold water could heal wounds and cure all ills. He treated his own fractured ribs with cold-water bandages and became convinced that this form of treatment was the future. His 'water-cure' consisted of various types of baths such as a half-bath, sitting bath, head bath, and a douche (cold water from a high spout directed onto the person *see Fig.23)*, it was accompanied by a strict diet and plenty of walks. He also treated some conditions by wrapping the patient in wet sheets and blankets, or encouraged sweating by covering the client with numerous blankets and a feather mattress. His methods became popular and he attracted a large clientele from all over Europe, many from high society. In 1842 Dr Wilson, who had been in practice for some years in England, visited Priessnitz, and was very impressed with what he witnessed. He returned to Malvern in Worcestershire, where he established his own 'Graefenburg House' to offer the 'water-cure', otherwise known as hydropathy. This proved to be very successful and his enterprise expanded, eventually consisting of two grand houses known as 'The Establishment' and 'Malvern House'. Great Malvern, like Bath, became a fashionable place to visit in order to take the waters and try alternative therapies.

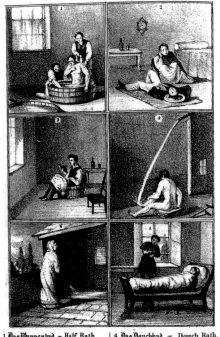

Fig. 23 Types of water-cure treatments
Wellcome Library

1. Das Wannenbad or Half Bath.
2. Das Kopfbad or Head Bath.
3. Das Sitzbad or Sitting Bath.
4. Das Douchbad or Douch Bath.
5. Das Schwitzen or Sweating.
6. Going to the Bath after Sweating.

Dr Charles Hastings (who was on the arsenic committee with Jonathan Toogood) was physician to the Worcester Infirmary at this time and was very scathing about the methods used by the hydropathists. Writing in the *Provincial Medical & Surgical Journal* in November 1842, he described the case of a 45 year-old woman who had occasionally attended the infirmary with generalised pain and attacks of difficulty with breathing. She decided to take herself off to the 'water-doctor', who assured her that she would be cured in a fortnight. For five weeks she suffered various forms of water treatments, minimal diet and nothing to drink except water or milk and water, by which time she was weak and emaciated and returned to the infirmary for relief. With care and nourishing food she returned home within the month. He comments that 'this is a notable instance of the application of the smothering and sweating bed-process to a poor, half-starved hypochondriacal woman, already brought into a great state of weakness and misery by poverty and wretchedness.' He goes on to say: 'to apply this same regimen to the cure of a poor, half-starved patient, [as opposed to a corpulent alderman] seems contrary to all rational treatment'.

τ

It was against this background of alternative cures that homeopathy arrived on the scene in the early part of the 19th century, and was to become the most controversial amongst the medical profession. Jonathan did not hold back with his criticisms of the homeopathic doctrines and expressed his views in a forthright manner: 'a system conceived in ignorance, and fostered by fraud and deceit.'

It was a German-born physician who founded a system of medicine with the principle that 'like cures like', which he named homeopathy. Samuel Hahnemann (1755-1843) from Meissen in Saxony was the son of a designer of porcelain. He became proficient in several languages and started life as a translator and only later studied medicine, obtaining his MD in 1779. He soon became disillusioned with orthodox medicine, which he later referred to as 'allopathic', believing that he was doing more harm than good, and so gave up his practice in 1784. He used his language skills to translate scientific and medical textbooks, and the story goes that while he was translating a treatise by William Cullen (an eminent Scottish physician), he came across the use of Peruvian bark (cinchona) for the treatment of malaria. He decided to investigate the effects of cinchona by conducting experiments on himself. After ingesting the bark, he actually developed the symptoms of malaria. From this he hypothesised that if any drug produced symptoms of a particular illness in a healthy individual, that same drug could be given to a patient already ill with those symptoms and then that patient would be cured. He undertook further experiments, convincing himself and others that his ideas would take medicine into a new era. These ideas of 'like curing like' were not altogether new, however, as Hippocrates had postulated a similar model.

Hahnemann then developed a method of diluting his new drugs in order to remove the toxic effects, but in order to make them effective, they had to undergo a technique of 'potentization', requiring further dilutions and 'succession' (vigorous shaking), in order to preserve their potency. He published his findings in a series of essays entitled *The Organon of the Healing Art* in 1810. This alternative therapy spread across Europe and reached America in 1825 where it rose in popularity, especially amongst the wealthy, the aristocracy and the clergy.

There were many critics of the homeopathic doctrines especially within the medical profession. Oliver Wendell Holmes, the American doctor who was ridiculed by some for his work on puerperal fever, repeated Hahnemann's experiments on Peruvian bark but was unable to reproduce the same results. He wrote a critical appraisal in 1842 – *Homeopathy and its Kindred Delusions*. James Young Simpson, the Scottish accoucheur, was also very critical, especially regarding the infinitesimal doses. But not everyone was quite so sceptical – Sir John Forbes, Queen Victoria's physician, expressed some interest, and in 1846 he wrote an essay entitled *Homeopathy, Allopathy and "Young Physic"*, taking a very measured approach to this new phenomenon. He admitted that allopathy 'does not cure a great proportion of the diseases it is supposed to cure and . . . until the proof is obtained, it behoves all who regard the prosperity and dignity of true art, to resist its progress'. He states what was true then and remains so in many ways today: 'the members of the medical profession at all times, and more especially in modern times, have been kept in a state of forced ignorance of the natural progress and event of diseases; in other words, of the natural history of disease in the human body.'

Despite its critics, a number of 'allopathic' doctors switched their allegiance to homeopathy, which caused a great deal of disquiet in the ranks of the medical profession. Writing *On the Doctrines of Homeopathy* in the *Provincial Medical & Surgical Journal* in April 1848, Dr Fairplay from Torquay made the comment:

> 'That many disorders, both acute and chronic, have been treated by these supposed remedies, that they have been the only medicinal means employed, and that such disorders have got well *after*, can readily be believed; but that any of such disorders have got well *in consequence*, or that they have even had the slightest effect on the cure, (physically) would, I think, puzzle the profoundest homeopathist to prove.'

He went on to criticise the past and present use of drugs of a 'poisonous nature' (such as arsenic and mercury) as well as the frequent use of venesection – 'a practice, I am happy to say, of late years much abated'. So he was not surprised that many people should have 'sought relief from such a depressing and destructive system, by rushing to the protection of the homeopathic doctor, who would relieve their disorders through the operation of faith, imagination, and globules.'

Jonathan Toogood was similarly forthright in his criticisms and in that same year published a 26-page leaflet entitled *Illustrations of The Fraud and Folly of Homeopathy*. This provoked the homeopathic journal to reply with a similarly long, but rather personal, rebuke. Jonathan argued that if the doctrines of Hahnemann were true, why had they not come to light in earlier generations? He also appreciated that many patients under the care of the medical profession 'are to be found amongst the nervous and hypochondriac' and he understood 'the powerful influence of the mind over disease' and the placebo effect. He went on to say of homeopaths: 'Such men basely take advantage of the fears of timid patients, and anxious parents, by magnifying trifling indispositions into serious diseases, declaring every hoarseness to be croup, and every pain in the head inflammation of the brain, and add them to their list of pretended cures with a total disregard of truth.'

He continued by giving examples of cases he had witnessed in his own practice. He talked of the involvement of the clergy and regretted their interference: 'It is, however, greatly to be lamented, that many are to be found amongst them who not only uphold this absurd and dangerous practice, but encourage it also by example.' Having seen such things as the Perkin's Tractors die a death, he believed that 'a few years only are wanting to complete the destiny of homeopathy'.

The homeopathists were quickly dismissive of Jonathan's 'rabid tirade' in his 'silly pamphlet' and in the following April an article entitled *Medical Toogoodism and Homeopathy* appeared in the *British Homeopathic Journal* (*Fig. 24 overleaf*).

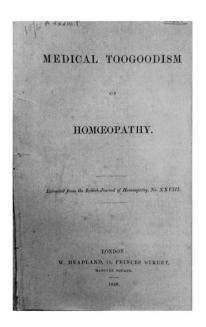

MEDICAL TOOGOODISM

AND

HOMŒOPATHY.

Extracted from the British Journal of Homœopathy, No. XXVIII.

LONDON:
W. HEADLAND, 15, PRINCES STREET,
HANOVER SQUARE.

1849.

Fig.24 Extract from British
Homeopathic Journal
April 1849
Dublin University

The first sentence of this 26-page rebuttal reads: 'There is something fatal in names'. The author gives examples of how certain names have been introduced into the English language to conjure up certain characteristics – Uncle Sam for an American and John Bull for an Englishman, and reminds us how Dr Guillotin's invention has left him with a 'sinister immortality'. The name Toogood, of course, is a gift to the writer, although he doubts that it's his real name: ' . . . so the word Toogoodism, derived from the name Jonathan Toogood, signifies that sturdy and unrelenting conviction of a class, or a profession, that its present holdings, prescriptive advantages, and prospective hopes are too good to allow for a moment the entertaining any proposal for any reform, or any important modification in its actual condition . . . Their old ways, their good ways, are always for them.' There then follows a long discussion defending homeopathy and its doctrines, and examples are given of those that condemn it 'without examination . . . This is the very essence of Toogoodism'.

τ

An incident had occurred some years earlier that would have influenced Jonathan's views regarding homeopathic practice and no doubt strengthened his negative attitude to those that indulge in this form of treatment. A woman presented to the Bridgwater Infirmary with a long-standing dislocated hip, which was confirmed by 'all the surgeons of the institution'. She had been under the care of a homeopathic doctor for some months, and explained that she had not been examined but had been assured that there was no disease present. Although attempts at the infirmary to treat the dislocation were put in place, it was felt that she would derive very little benefit at this stage and would 'always be a cripple'. At the end of three weeks she left the Infirmary. Three months later Jonathan received a letter from the homeopath's attorney, charging him with defamation of character, as the woman claimed that she had been told by Jonathan that 'her hip was out; the homeopath was a fool; that she had been improperly treated; and she might have been cured in a fortnight.' Jonathan denied that he had used such language, but despite this the case was brought before the court at Taunton assizes, 'before a judge, a great favourer of homeopathy'. Despite a one-sided address by the judge, Jonathan was acquitted but the affair had cost him £100 in legal expenses.

τ

By the 1850s the medical profession was becoming very nervous about the number of orthodox practitioners switching their allegiance to homeopathy. Writing to the editor of the *Provincial Medical & Surgical Journal* in July 1851, Dr John Rose Cormack suggested that a broad line should be drawn between medicine and homeopathy, and called on the Provincial Medical and Surgical Association (PMSA) to enforce such a demarcation: 'Let the Association declare that the names of the homeopathic practitioners, and of those who hold professional intercourse with them, cannot be on its list of members'.

At the 19th Anniversary meeting of the PMSA held in Brighton on 13th and 14th August 1851, the President Dr Charles Hastings, in his address, outlined the concerns that homeopathy was being practised by some of their members, and suggested the appointment of a small committee to review membership of such individuals. Dr Cormack from London, Dr Tunstall from Bath and Dr Ranking from Norwich were appointed. Among other recommendations, they proposed excluding from the association three classes of practitioners who practise – a) homeopathy alone; b) a combination of all types of unorthodox treatment; or c) hold 'professional intercourse' with homeopathic practitioners. These proposals were discussed and unanimously agreed and a year later the report of the Committee on Irregular Practice was read out by Dr Cormack, which recommended 'bye-laws' that embraced the above proposals. The report was received and adopted.

τ

Whatever the reader's views concerning alternative and complementary medicine, it is fair to say that the debate continues today. In July 2015 The *British Medical Journal* printed the views of two leading academics on either side of the argument, under the title *Should doctors recommend homeopathy?* Despite the fact that there is no sound scientific basis behind homeopathy, it continues to be used as an alternative treatment by many individuals and there are four Homeopathic Hospitals in Britain – in London, Bristol, Liverpool and Glasgow. The one thing we are sure about is that Jonathan was quite wrong with his prophecy that the practice would come to an end within a few years, and one can only guess as to what his reaction would have been, if he had known that the doctrines were still being aired two centuries later.

Chapter 13

Family

I am thankful to enjoy good health, after forty years most laborious country practice, and gratefully acknowledge that my profession has enabled me to educate, and establish in respectable positions in life, eight sons

Jonathan Toogood 1853

Anyone who has attempted to research their own family history will know just how difficult and confusing it can be at times. Ancestral sites on the internet certainly help in the search but there often remain tantalizing gaps which frustratingly cannot be filled – the person you wish to find disappears off the radar! This is the case with the Toogoods. Like most Victorian families, theirs was a large one, as was that of Jonathan's wife Ann (Giles). At the beginning of this book the author has provided the reader with family trees, which hopefully will aid with names and dates.

All of Jonathan and Ann's children were born in Bridgwater. It is unknown as to whether Jonathan helped at his wife's confinements but we have already seen him travelling out to Mark to attend to his sister-in-law. Like many couples at that time, Jonathan and Ann experienced the death of children in infancy – seventh son Francis was baptised on February 9th 1821 but died 3 months later; ninth son Frederic lived for only a month in 1824; last child Mary Ann (b1829) also very sadly died in April 1831. All three children were buried at Mark, their mother's childhood home. Jonathan and Ann must have felt these losses very deeply and they probably contributed to Jonathan's empathy towards his patients. There is one other child who remains elusive – Frances, their fourth child and first daughter (b1814); she may well have married and changed her name but there are no records to support this that the author has found.

We see from the quote at the beginning of this chapter that Jonathan was very proud that he had educated eight sons, all of whom prospered in their chosen careers:

Jonathan James Toogood, their eldest child and known to the family as James, was 9 months older than his cousin John Allen Giles (son of William Giles, Ann's brother - *see Plate 32*). They were playmates as children and their close relationship continued into old age. From time to time James would go over to Southwick House in Mark for a week or two and they would get up to mischief. On one occasion John Allen Giles described how James Toogood had thrown an oyster shell at him, cutting open his head. Five years later when they were at Dorchester Grammar School together, the Headmaster, Mr Evan Davies noticed a scar on John's head and learned that James was responsible. Believing this to be a recent event, he was about to flog him, when the boys explained that it had occurred 5 years earlier! James himself suffered a fractured collarbone as a baby and broke it again at the age of 10, but this did not deter him from participating in sports later on. He was keen on all games, especially football, and gained a number of prizes.

*Plate 32 John Allen Giles,
academic and writer
(1808-84)*

John Allen Giles spent time in Bridgwater staying at the Toogoods' house with his cousins and writes of going to North Petherton Fair and also Saint Matthew's Fair, where he witnessed bull-baiting in 1813 at the tender age of 5. The bull escaped! He also watched a man put in a pillory from the window of his uncle Toogood's house, 'which commanded a view of The Cornhill up towards West Street' – the poor man being subjected to missiles comprised of rotten eggs, cabbages and mud amongst other things. John Allen Giles tells of another episode in that house when he was being brought downstairs in the arms of an aunt (*he doesn't say which one*) and fell back over the banisters, only being saved by the aunt grabbing at the long clothes he was still wearing at that time. James Toogood also spent time at his uncle Robert Giles' house in Burnham with his cousins William and John Allen Giles, the latter describing uncle Robert as 'one of the kindest of men'.

Before attending Dorchester Grammar with his cousin, James Toogood had previously spent time at the grammar school in Bridgwater. After 2 years at Dorchester, he moved on to Exeter Grammar School and from there, at the age of 14, he entered the headmaster's house at Harrow. In 1826 he went up to Balliol College, Oxford where he became a good oarsman and was selected for the first ever boat race against Cambridge University at Henley in June 1829. This university match was proposed by Mr Snow of St John's, Cambridge to Mr Staniforth of Christ Church, Oxford in March of that year – the two men had been schoolfellows at Eton. The race took place on 10th June. Oxford had the heavier crew in a boat built by Stephen Davis, which was a good 2ft shorter than that used by Cambridge. James weighed in at 14st 10lb and rowed at number 5. A letter, sent to the Cambridge boat the week before, described each member of the Oxford crew. After Toogood's name, it was written – '[Toogood] for you: but just the man for us'. The crew wore dark blue striped jerseys with black straw hats and handkerchiefs and canvas trousers, and their boat was green. According to the female spectators, they were 'powerful, well grown and good looking men'. The Cambridge crew was dressed in white with pink handkerchiefs and the boat was also pink. It was a perfect day and it was estimated that about 20,000 people watched the race, which was won by Oxford. Over half a century later there was a commemoration banquet to mark the first Oxford and Cambridge boat race which James attended, wearing his original race jersey.

Fig.25
Oxford Boat
1829

James met his wife Harriet Lovell about this time. Harriet's uncle was Edmund Lovell, the Archdeacon of Bath. In 1832 James was ordained at Corfe with a stipend of £40 and became engaged to Harriet. They were married in September 1834 and initially set up home in Castle Street in Bridgwater, where their daughters Alice and Ann were born. However, that same year his father Jonathan bought the living for James at North Petherton church (2 miles south of Bridgwater) for £800, stipulating that the stipend should be £140, but James ran into some financial difficulties in his early days due to his generous nature, subscribing to every local charity and good cause. James was very hospitable when he eventually moved to the vicarage – probably a little too extravagant on many occasions. When he took over from the Revd William George, he found the church affairs to be very unsatisfactory. Revd George had been unpopular and was known to be mean. The vicarage was in need of urgent repair and the Church had been neglected. Its roof in particular was in a bad state – on one occasion when James was up on the roof inspecting its condition, it collapsed and he fell 9 feet, fortunately catching hold of some scaffolding before reaching the ground, no doubt testimony to his fitness and strength. The choir and bell-ringers were in disarray and he drew up rules for the ringers, implementing small fines for drunkenness, swearing and non-attendance. Along with the church renovations, the organ was restored.

Like his father Jonathan and his grandfather and his great-grandfather on the Toogood side, James took his duties to the poor very seriously. He established a free day school in 1836 for parents who could not afford any school fees. Within a year it had 90 pupils, who were taught reading, needlework and religious studies. He also set up a penny club in order to provide blankets for the poor and needy. In 1837 he worked hard to secure funds from the Treasury and elsewhere to build a National School in North Petherton, Lord Portman contributing to this cause. In 1836 he had set up a new Friendly Society at the George Inn in the village, named the North

Petherton Friendly Society and by 1837 it had 74 members, his wife presenting them with a crimson banner. He took on the role of rural dean and Inspector of Schools and was known to be rather officious if any irregularities were found, his main aim being to improve unsatisfactory conditions – yet another Toogood trait!

As a young man, he enjoyed taking part in the local hunt on his horse named 'Forrester' which had been a gift from his father, and he took great interest in the local ploughing matches. In 1850 he left North Petherton to become rector at St Andrew's Church in Holborn, London, which was no doubt a great contrast from his life in Somerset. In 1858, however, he transferred to Kirkby Overblow in the Yorkshire Dales, once again a rural setting. He remained there until his death in 1892. He did not lose touch with his family and it is obvious from letters that there were often family gatherings. James gives us a glimpse of his father Jonathan as a family man, describing him as being 'always most kind and liberal'. He makes the observation: 'we all have much cause to be thankful for the excellent education that he gave us, and the readiness with which he assented to schemes for our amusement.'

τ

Jonathan's next two sons, Isaac Baruch Toogood and John Giles Toogood, both entered the medical profession. It is unclear whether they were apprenticed to their father but they, like him, went on to study at St Bartholomew's Hospital. The records of pupils attending the medical school are said not to be reliable for the early part of the 19th century and their names unfortunately do not appear on the lists. However, John Allen Giles recalls calling on his cousins Baruch and John at the hospital in 1829 and being taken to the dissecting rooms 'where there was a fearful smell from the several bodies lying on the table'. Two years later Baruch was back in Bridgwater at the Infirmary as the apothecary dispensing the medicines. He obtained his MRCS and LSA in 1833 and then went to Torquay to set up a successful practice. He and his wife Ann had two sons – Frederick became a solicitor, while Seymour reached the rank of Lieutenant Colonel in the Royal Artillery.

Third son John G Toogood was elected to the office of surgeon at Bridgwater in 1833 and continued to work there for many years. He was also one of the surgeons at the Bridgwater Eye Dispensary in Victoria Street, founded by his father Jonathan in 1834, and he was still listed as working there along with John Parsons in 1847. The dispensary was absorbed into the Infirmary in 1850. It was sited in Victoria Street – the latter no longer exists, although it appears that it was somewhere between King's Place and King's Square.

As a boy, John Toogood had also played with his cousins at Southwick House and on one occasion caused consternation by disappearing for two hours, after committing some 'crime'. He was found in the corn-bin in the stable! John married Elizabeth Hiron, the daughter of Thomas Hiron a surgeon in Warwickshire in 1840. There were no children from this marriage and in the 1851 census John is described as a widower. In 1855

Jonathan wrote to Bridgwater Infirmary explaining that his son was 'temporarily incapacitated from his duties'. A further letter offered his resignation, although the infirmary postponed this for three months, presumably because he was a valued member of the staff. Twenty years later, at the age of 66, while staying with his brother James in Kirkby Overblow, John went for a walk one morning but very sadly did not return – he was found drowned in a small river in the neighbourhood. The coroner's inquest confirmed the cause of death to be suicide following a long period of depression, the death certificate stating 'Melancholia above 20 years' – a sad end to the life of a successful surgeon.

Jonathan's fourth son, Charles Toogood was born in 1815 and also trained in London as a surgeon. He is recorded as a surgeon superintendent on board the ship 'Persia' sailing from London to Tasmania in 1835. In Sydney he probably met Jane Mary Dulhunty, the daughter of Dr John Dulhunty, a wealthy naval surgeon who had previously emigrated to Australia from his home in Devon. Charles and Jane returned to England and were married in North Petherton in 1840 and it is quite likely that his brother Jonathan James officiated at their marriage. Their son Charles Henry Lawrence Toogood was born in 1844 in Westbury-on-Trym near Bristol. By 1858, however, Charles was back in Australia, running a medical practice in the bush at Bundarra in New South Wales. Sadly Jane died there in 1858, as did Charles the following year. Their son Charles was therefore orphaned at the age of 15 and in the 1861 census he is recorded at a boarding school in Weston-super-Mare. It is quite possible that he lived with his grandfather Jonathan in Torquay until adulthood, when he moved to London. When Jonathan wrote his will in 1859, he made provision for this grandson.

The next sons Henry (b.1817) and William (b.1819) both entered the legal profession. Written agreements between Jonathan and attorneys John Miller and Thomas Walker still exist, dated 1835 and 1838 respectively, and were drawn up at No.3 Furnival's Inn in the City of London, regarding Henry and William. Furnival's Inn (see Fig.24 overleaf) was founded as one of the nine inns of chancery in 1383 but the medieval building was demolished in 1818. A new block of apartments was built on the original site in 1828 and still housed members of the legal profession. One notable occupant was Charles Dickens, who lived there between 1833 and 1836 – one wonders whether Henry bumped into Charles Dickens on occasions! Henry remained in London and with his wife Frances lived in Kensington, where they had four children (three daughters and one son). William remained a bachelor and is recorded living with his brother Isaac Baruch in Torquay in both the 1851 and 1861 censuses.

Fig.26 Furnival's Inn as depicted by Shepherd 1828

Next came Octavius (b.1823), whom John Allen Giles describes as a 'funny little fellow' when he was a child. In 1840 he was one of John Allen's pupils at Windlesham Hall in Bagshot, studying for the entry exam to Haileybury College but he struggled with his studies, failed the examination and returned to Bridgwater. He joined the Indian Army and was involved in the Santal Rebellion in 1855 – the Santals were an indigenous people who had seen their lands captured. Octavius married twice and had two sons, one from each marriage. He spent his retirement years in Kensington and according to John Allen Giles suffered with heart problems.

Alexander Decimus was Jonathan's youngest son born in 1826 and, like Octavius, took the military route. He became a Captain in the 2nd Bengal Fusiliers and married Georgina Warry of Shapwick House in Shapwick, Somerset, and together they had four children. Their only son Cecil served in the Boer War and later in 1914 as a Major in the 1st Battalion Lincolnshire Regiment, when he was shot and reported missing. Fortunately he survived, having undergone surgery at the hospital at Paderborn, a German POW camp. He was promoted to Lieutenant Colonel in 1918 and in 1921 was serving in Poona, India. It was here that he received the news that his son Harold had been kidnapped and executed by the IRA. Cecil blamed the Army for poor security and resigned his commission – another example perhaps of a Toogood standing by his principles.

τ

This then is the story of Jonathan's eight sons and it is the oldest son James who gives us a good insight into Jonathan's role as a father. In a letter to John Allen Giles in 1841 James again recalls Jonathan's generosity. He asks his cousin for advice concerning the taking on of two pupils to boost his meagre income of £140 earned from his curacy. He writes: '…'tis true I spend more than that, as you may suppose, but the £140 is all I can call my own; the residue proceeds from my Father, who is very liberal, but as he has many ways for his money, and works hard for it, I think I ought to do something myself if I can.'

There is no doubt that Jonathan cared for his family and provided for all his sons in the best way he could, namely by securing them all a good education. In return, later in life Isaac Baruch advanced his father a sum of money to enable him to purchase a house in Torquay and this is recognised in Jonathan's will. All his grandchildren appeared to have prospered too and his granddaughters married well. James, his eldest son remarks in 1880 in another letter to John Allen Giles: 'I have my grandsons with me; one is at Keble [College, Oxford] – a nice lad. I have 20 grandchildren – I hope out of them all, some will be useful at all events'.

In summary, this was a family of achievers, who looked out for one another and remained supportive to each other throughout their lives. Perhaps there is something in the name TOOGOOD after all.

Chapter 14

Legacy

In every situation of life our primary enquiry ought to be what is right to be done, and having ascertained as far as we have the power, we must then perform or endure it.   John Abernethy in a letter to Jonathan Toogood

In November 1845 the management committee at Bridgwater Infirmary received the following letter: –

Ashley Lodge, Torquay,
November 25th, 1845

As it is my intention to reside at this place during the Winter, I beg to resign my situation of Physician and Surgeon to your excellent charity.

Upwards of thirty years have elapsed since with your assistance I was enabled to found the Bridgwater Infirmary, and during that period it has been my unceasing endeavour to render it useful, by devoting my constant care and attention to those entrusted to my charge.

I thank you sincerely for the invariable confidence you have reposed in me, with my best wishes for its prosperity.

I remain,

(Signed) Jonathan Toogood.

His resignation was received with 'extreme regret' but the Committee wished to communicate to Dr Toogood through the Chairman 'their deep sense of gratitude for the energy and talent, the high professional skill and unwearied industry with which he has discharged the duties of that office [Physician and Surgeon] during the 33 years that he has been connected with this Institution.' Jonathan did, however, agree to take on the role of Consulting Physician and Surgeon to the Infirmary.

A life-size portrait of Jonathan was painted by a William Baker, a resident of Bridgwater, and was presented to the Committee by the Revd Noel Ellison, the Rector of Huntspill in December 1845. Subscribers to the Infirmary from the town and neighbourhood commissioned and paid for the painting. It was hung in the entrance hall of the hospital, under which a brass plaque was inscribed:

Plate 33 Brass plaque Bridgwater Infirmary
Photo by Jenny McCubbin

Presented to the Bridgwater Infirmary by Subscribers to this Institution, whose names are recorded in the minutes of December 29th 1845, as a testimony of their grateful sense of gratuitous and highly valuable services of Jonathan Toogood, Esq, M.D., to this Institution for a period of more than 30 years.

Plate 34 Sketch of
Jonathan Toogood
No date

In addition to Jonathan's main work at the Infirmary and his own practice, it must be remembered that he also established in 1834 the Bridgwater Eye Dispensary in Victoria Street. He funded this institution himself and his son John Giles Toogood, as we have already seen, was one of the surgeons there. The types of eye conditions that needed attention were cataracts, ocular infections, injuries, glaucoma and squints. Cataracts were treated by a procedure called 'couching', a technique dating back to antiquity. This was a quick, relatively painless procedure which had overall good results, although, of course, prior to the introduction of antisepsis, post-operative inflammation could lead to further problems. A small incision was made with a couching needle and the lens was pushed into the vitreous humour, thereby displacing the opaque lens and allowing light into the eye. It is noteworthy that the Eye Dispensary was opened one year after the notable smallpox epidemic in the town. Smallpox can scar and damage the eyes, and was a common cause of blindness at the time.

Ophthalmology was to come into its own in the 19th century and the surgeons of the day were experimenting with new techniques. Throughout the centuries cataract surgery had often been undertaken by itinerant quacks and charlatans, and a tightening up of this haphazard system was overdue. In 1804, encouraged by Sir Astley Cooper, John Cunningham Saunders (1773-1810), one of the new pioneering surgeons experimenting with cataract surgery, founded the eye dispensary in London, which became known as Moorfields Eye Hospital. This set in motion the establishment of eye dispensaries around the country, the west of England leading the way with centres such as Bath and Bristol. There were 19 hospitals founded between 1808 and 1832. James Billet established and funded the Taunton Eye Hospital in 1816 and continued as the sole surgeon there until 1865. Bridgwater was in the second wave of 15 dispensaries set up between 1834 and 1861. Once again Jonathan was ahead of the game compared with many parts of England, and Bridgwater was the beneficiary.

Further developments in eye treatment were made possible, when in 1850 Hermann von Helmholtz (1821-1894), a German physician and physicist, produced the first ophthalmoscope, or 'eye mirror' as it was first called. This was to give a whole new perspective to ophthalmology.

τ

Jonathan continued to practise medicine after his resignation from Bridgwater at the age of 61. In fact he was often seen attending patients with his son Isaac Baruch in Torquay. In 1845 he published a pamphlet entitled *Hints to Mothers and other persons interested in the management of females at the age of puberty*. This 19-page leaflet covers the symptoms and signs of chlorosis, giving examples of several cases. Some patients had successfully been treated by him, but others unfortunately had a fatal outcome. Chlorosis was a condition about which Jonathan was passionate (*see Chapter 6*). His article, however, received poor reviews from the medical profession, the *Medical-Chirurgical Review* in July 1845 commenting: 'Surely not what the profession has a right to expect from so respectable a member of their corps as Dr. Toogood'. More damning was the review in *The Lancet*, concerned that his words were more likely 'to frighten the mothers to whom the hints were addressed'; and it is true that the descriptions of the disease and post-mortem findings are very graphic. The journal goes on to say: 'Dr Toogood is treading on dangerous ground . . . he lays himself open to the charge of having written it merely to be able to advertise himself at the same time'. The pamphlet was advertised in *Woolmer's Exeter and Plymouth Gazette* and was certainly aimed at the general public. He may well have over-reached himself on this occasion, even allowing for different sensitivities at that time, but there appears to be no doubt that his intention was to inform and perhaps prevent a condition that was prevalent: 'having witnessed so much misery and so many fatal consequences from warnings having been neglected, which would have claimed the earliest and most anxious attention, if their importance had been known, I am strongly impressed with the duty of stating, that conviction which is the result of considerable experience.' He concludes by urging mothers to pay particular attention to their daughter's health. It is difficult for us in the 21st century to comprehend just what a devastating condition chlorosis was at this period in history.

τ

Although Jonathan had moved to Torquay on leaving Bridgwater, he did spend time working in other places until his eventual retirement. In the 1851 census, for example, he is shown living in London at 94 Wimpole Street, which is only a stone's throw from Harley Street. His occupation is listed as 'physician' and it is very likely that he was still practising at this time. This is the year that the Sale of Arsenic Act went onto the statute book.

There is some thin evidence that he also practised in Taunton. His nephew by marriage, Charles Edmund Giles, (John Allen Giles' brother) an ecclesiastical architect, is shown in the 1851 census living at 14 The Crescent. There is some correspondence from Jonathan written from The Crescent in 1853. Whether he was just visiting his nephew or actually had a consulting room at this address remains unclear. Certainly his book *Reminiscences of a Medical Life* was printed in Taunton in that same year.

τ

Jonathan's abiding legacy, however, remains the Bridgwater Infirmary, which continued to prosper, as Jonathan had hoped and expressed in his resignation letter. Although the number of changes that took place over the following 100 years are too many to list in this context, it would be amiss not to mention just a few significant additions. In 1847 a new operating theatre, bathroom and female ward, along with a new room for the matron and a 'modern' laundry, were added at a cost of £428-14s-5d; the 'Friends' of the infirmary covered the entire sum. Two years later the Infirmary responded well to a severe cholera epidemic, when 1,000 cases were treated. In 1864 a special appeal to the general public was set up in order to purchase the adjoining house - £339 was collected.

Plate 35 The Bridgwater Infirmary in 1865
Blake Museum

Further alterations took place in 1871, when hot and cold water services were added to the wards and a lift was installed. By 1877 the layout of the Infirmary was set out as described below:

Ground floor – Entrance hall with stone staircase and gallery, house surgeon's sitting room, committee room, waiting room, 3 consulting rooms, a surgery, 2 small isolation wards, matron's room, domestic offices and laundry.

First floor – 3 wards, operating room adjacent to surgical ward, a women's day-room, bedrooms for the house surgeon, matron and 2 nurses.

Second floor – female ward (Poole Ward, named after Mr G.S.Poole who had served as Chairman of the Committee for over 30 years), nurses' sitting rooms and bedrooms and servants' bedrooms.

The Infirmary was now able to accommodate 40 in-patients. A portico at the front of the Infirmary was added in 1876 as a memorial to Mr. Poole.

Plate 36 Infirmary with added portico *author's photo 2013*

In the 1880s Mr James Broadmead of Glastonbury gave land, valued at £7,375, to the infirmary in order that the establishment could benefit from the rents; this would have been seen as a very generous contribution. In 1887 Mr Francis Thompson donated a freehold dwelling next door, which was let out to bring in additional income. By 1887 all nurses had undergone training and held certificates of their qualification. In 1890, 76 years on from its establishment, the Infirmary had treated a total of 11,621 in-patients and 73,793 out-patients.

By the end of the 19th century the Infirmary was more commonly referred to as 'Bridgwater Hospital' but it was running into financial difficulties again, despite the various contributions made by its benefactors, and steps were taken to recruit new subscribers from the surrounding parishes. Fund-raising continued throughout the next four decades until it was taken over by the state in 1948. Concerts, fairs and carnivals were organised but it was the generosity of local people that kept the hospital afloat.

Despite its financial constraints the hospital kept abreast with the latest equipment and in 1902 the first X-ray apparatus was purchased. Wilhelm Roentgen (1845-1923) a German physicist, first published his work on the discovery of X-rays in December 1885, so this type of equipment was still in its infancy. By 1921 the hospital had one of the most up to date X-ray machines in the region and in 1933 a whole new department was opened. In 1904 a telephone was installed and 6 years later the gas lamps were replaced by electric lighting.

1914 saw the start of the First World War and the committee agreed to place twelve beds at the disposal of the military for war casualties. The matron at this time, Miss Keating, later received recognition from the war office for her work in nursing the war wounded. A new wing to the hospital was added in 1914 and the first female house surgeon was appointed in October of that year. The war gave women doctors the opportunity to gain hospital appointments, the men having been called up to serve on the front line.

The hospital continued to receive generous donations and the town gave support to appeals for money. Every organization became involved and monies were raised through such events as dances, pantomimes, football matches, fêtes and whist drives. There was even a brass slot at the entrance to the infirmary where donations could be posted. The 'Hospital League' managed to raise a total of £20,000 in tuppences, collected from the people over the course of 14 years.

Plate 37 Fundraising coin slot
Photo by Jenny McCubbin

In 1940 an 'iron lung' was donated to be used for the sufferers of polio, which in the 20th century had become a serious concern especially among children – the first polio vaccines didn't appear until the 1950s.

In January 1948 the Chairman of the management committee reported that the Regional Board was making plans to link up hospitals in the country. The last Annual Meeting (131st) of annual subscribers to the Infirmary was held on July 1st 1948, just a few days before the hospital passed into the hands of the state.

The Infirmary building remains a familiar sight alongside the River Parrett in the town but the hospital itself moved in 2014 into modern new premises just outside the town and has become a community hospital with out-patient, physiotherapy, X-ray and minor injury departments along with 30 in-patient beds.

Plate 38 The new Bridgwater Hospital opened in 2014
Author's photo

Over the years the portrait of Jonathan Toogood sadly seems to have been lost but the plaque accompanying the painting has now been transferred to the new hospital, along with many dedications to other medical staff and committee members, who worked tirelessly to allow the institution to prosper for over two hundred years.

Jonathan eventually settled into retirement in Torquay and it was here that he died at No.2 Abbey Crescent on December 7th 1870 at the age of 86. His death was registered at Newton Abbott, his death certificate gave the cause of death as 'Old Age'. His house in Abbey Crescent later became part of the Palm Court Hotel but this has since been demolished and replaced by luxury apartments. In his will he provided for his wife Ann, his sons and his orphaned grandson Charles Isaac Lawrence Toogood. Ann lived on for another five years and paid visits to all her sons. In the 1871 census she is staying with her brother Joseph Giles in Wells. She was always described as being in good health.

Having received the news of Jonathan's death, the Management Committee at Bridgwater Infirmary conveyed their 'sincere sympathy' to Mrs. Toogood and expressed to her their high appreciation of 'the eminent services during the active portion of his life he had rendered to their Institution, and their deep sense of gratitude for the same.'

τ

Jonathan Toogood was not without his faults, of course, and some of his grandfather John's traits filtered down through the family, resulting in Jonathan ruffling a few feathers on occasions. There is no doubt that his intentions were sincere. Overall he was respected by his colleagues in the medical profession and was (more importantly) spoken about warmly by his family. His main achievement has to be the Bridgwater Infirmary, however, and one hopes that he would have been pleased with the improvements made to the institution in the subsequent years after his death. The scientific and technological advances that began at the end of the 19th century completely changed the whole ethos of the hospital system. No longer were hospitals meant for the poor – their role was to serve the whole community, rich and poor.

One can only guess as to how Jonathan would feel today about all the advancements that have been made in medical science in the last 100 years. To be able to treat and relieve diseases that once would have resulted in a fatal outcome would no doubt have given him great satisfaction. The 'art' of medicine is fast disappearing in this technological and digital world and along with this some of the compassion that medical practitioners such as Jonathan had in abundance. What we gain on one hand, we lose with the other. Having said that, one thing is abundantly clear – that no one would wish to return to 19th century practices and we have to applaud the medical profession at that time for their achievements in such difficult circumstances.

Jonathan Toogood certainly immersed himself in his profession and it seems fitting to end this book with his own words, which sum up his passion for medical practice:

'From general and personal experience, I would recommend my professional brethren never to retire from their active duties whilst their mental faculties and physical strength remain unimpaired, from a conviction that those who adopt such a determination will best consult their own health and happiness.'

References, Bibliography and Further Reading

Toogood, J (1853). *Reminiscences of a Medical Life* London: Longman & Co.

Chapter 1 – A Sherborne Family
- Osborn, Bob. (2016) *Markes Lambe*. Available at http://www.yeovilhistory.info Search Listings 'L'. Last accessed 10/3/2017
- Penn, Ray. *A Short History of Sherborne*. Museum Abstracts, No. 17; Sherborne Museum
- The Sherborne Register 1550-1950 (4th ed., 1950); The Old Shirburnian Society
- Gourley, A.B (1951). *The History of Sherborne School*. Winchester: Warren & Sons.
- Medlycott, M (2008). *Somerset and Dorset Notes and Queries. 43. John Toogood of Sherborne (1713-1795)*
- Toogood, John. Memorandum Book. Dorset History Centre. D170/1
- *Oxford University Alumni, 1500-1886* [database on-line]. Available: http://search.ancestry.co.uk/cgi-bin/sse.dll?ti=5538&indiv=try&db=oxfordalum&h=361001
- Kington Magna. http://www.dorsetlife.co.uk/2006/12/kington-magna
- Toogood, J. *Letters to the gentlemen, clergy, and freeholders of the county of Dorset.* Sherborne: Goadby, Lerpiniere, and Langdon. (2nd ed.). ECCO print edition. Reproduction from British Library
- Clarkson, T (1808). *The History of The Abolition of the African Slave Trade by the British Parliament*. Vol. 1. London: Longman, Hurst, Rees & Orme. p425.
- Scott,R (1821). The late Rev. Charles Toogood, *The Monthly Repository of Theology*, January to December incl. 1821, Vol xvi pp 719-720

Chapter 2 – Starting Out
- Woolrich, A P. (2011) *Robert Anstice 1757-1845*. Available at http://www.bridgwaterscientists.org.uk/anstice/ Last accessed 10/3/2017
- Bynum, W F (1994). *Science and the Practice of Medicine in the Nineteenth Century*. 8th ed. New York: Cambridge University Press.
- Porter, R (1997). *The Greatest Benefit to Mankind*. London: HarperCollins.
- Lane, J (2001). *A Social History of Medicine*. London: Routledge.
- Corfield, J. *From Poison Peddlers to Civic Worthies: The Reputation of the Apothecaries in Georgian England*. 2009. Social History of Medicine Vol 22, No 1 pp1-21
- Macilwain, G (1853). *Memoirs of John Abernethy*. London: Hatchard and Co. (Classic Reprint Series, Forgotten Books)
- Auden, Rita. (1978). A Hunterian pupil. Sir William Blizard and The London Hospital. *Annals of the Royal College of Surgeons of England. Vol 60, pp345-349.*
- Blizard Institute – available at http://www.blizard.qmul.ac.uk Search 'About ' listings. Last accessed 10/3/2017
- Richardson, R (1988). *Death, Dissection and the Destitute*. Paperback edition 2001. London: Phoenix Press.
- Wise, S (2005). *The Italian Boy*. 2nd ed. London: Pimlico, Random House.
- RCS Plarr's Lives of the Fellows at http://livesonline.rcseng.ac.uk   Search Toogood, J

Chapter 3 – Return to Bridgwater

- The Kings Candlesticks: Pedigrees. Available at
http://www.thekingscandlesticks.com/webs/pedigrees   Last accessed 14/3/2017
- Parrish, P (2002). *The History of Wilton Gaol, Taunton, Somerset.* The Somerset &
Dorset Family History Society.
- Education in Bridgwater. Available at http://www.british-
history.ac.uk/vch/som/vol6/pp238-241   Last accessed 14/3/2017
- Giles, J A. *Diary & Memoirs.* Held at Somerset Heritage Centre
- Lawrence, J F (2005). *A History of Bridgwater.* Chichester: Phillimore & Co. Ltd.
- Squibbs, P J (1968). *A Bridgwater Diary 1800-1967.* Bridgwater: Squibbs.
- Evans, R (2012). *The Book of Bridgwater.* 2nd ed. Wellington: Halsgrove.
- Woolrich, T. (2013). Public Health and Water Supply in Bridgwater, Somerset. (Parts
2 – 4)
- Powell, A H (1908). *Bridgwater in the Later Days.* Bridgwater: Page & Son. 150-168

Chapter 4 – The Art of Medicine

- Porter, R (1997). *The Greatest Benefit to Mankind.* London: Harper Collins.
- Bynum, W F (2008). *The History of Medicine - A very Short Introduction.* New York:
Oxford University Press. Chapter 1.
- Jackson, L (2015). *Dirty Old London.* Yale University Press.
- Mackenzie, J. *Counter-irritation.* Proceedings of the Royal Society of Medicine
(Therapeutical and Pharmacological Section). 1909; 2. 75-80
- Toogood, J. *On the efficacy of counter-irritation in some affections of the brain.* Prov
Med Surg J 1846; s1-10:77
- Smart, J. *Effects of Miasma.* Prov Med Surg J 1844; s1-8: 559
- *Burial in Towns.* Prov Med Surg J. 1843; s1-10: 235
- Squibbs, P J (1968). *A Bridgwater Diary 1800-1967.* Bridgwater: Squibbs.
- Theodore Williams, C. (1907). *Laennec and the Evolution of the Stethoscope.* BMJ. Vol
2 (issue 2427), 6-7.
- Porter, R (1989). *Quacks. Fakers & Charlatans in Medicine.* 4th ed. Stroud,
Gloucestershire: Tempus Publishing Limited.

Chapter 5 – General Practice, Surgery and the advent of Anaesthesia

- Baxby, D (1994). *Vaccination Jenner's Legacy.* Berkley: Jenner Educational Trust.
- Green, M. *Cod liver oil and tuberculosis.* BMJ 2011;343:d7505
- Toogood, J. *On the administration of cod-liver oil in tubercular diseases of the lungs.*
Prov Med Surg J 1846; s1-10:488
- Everett, D. *On the use of cod-liver oil in tubercular disease.* Prov Med Surg J 1846; s1-
10: 538
- Toogood, J. *Cod-liver oil in phthisis. Dr Ranking's inquiries.* Prov Med Surg J 1849; s1-
13: 300
- Ellis, H (2009). *The Cambridge Illustrated History of Surgery.* 2nd ed. New York:
Cambridge University Press.
- *Breast Cancer in 1811: Fanny Burney's Account of her Mastectomy.* (2010). Available:
http://newjacksonianblog.blogspot.co.uk/2010/12/breast-cancer-in-1811-fanny-
burneys.html Last accessed 10/3/2017.
- Snow, S (2008). *Blessed Days of Anaesthesia.* Oxford: Oxford University Press.

Chapter 6 – Childbirth and the Cheshire Cat

- Donnison, J (1988). *Midwives and Medical Men*. 2nd ed. New Barnet, Herts: Historical Publications Ltd.
- Hunter, K. *Dr John Clarke: licentiate in midwifery of the Royal College of Physicians of London*. Clin Med JRCPL 2002;2: 153-6
- Wendell Holmes, O. (1843). *Contagiousness of Puerperal Fever*. Dodo Press.
- Simpson, J Y. *Discovery of a new anaesthetic agent more efficient than sulphuric ether*. Prov Med Surg J 1847; s1-11: 656
- Snow J. *On the administration of Chloroform during parturition*. Assoc Med J 1853; s3-1: 500
- Beecroft, S. *Objections to the use of Chloroform*. Assoc Med J 1853; s3-1: 524
- Pickford, J. *Injurious effects of the inhalation of ether*. Prov Med Surg J 1847; s1-11: 330
- Louden, I S L. (1980). Chlorosis, anaemia, and anorexia nervosa. BMJ. Vol.281 (20-27 December), pp. 1669-1675.
- Correspondence re Chlorosis, anaemia and anorexia nervosa. Br Med J (Clin Res Ed) 1981; 282: 228 and 1981; 282: 906
- Stockman, R. *Observations on the causes and treatment of Chlorosis*. Br Med J 1895; 2: 1473

Chapter 7 – Bridgwater Infirmary

- Rawcliffe, C (1999). *Medicine & Society*. 2nd ed. London: Sandpiper Books Ltd.
- Orme,N and Webster,M (1995). *The English Hospital 1070-1570*. London: Yale University Press. pp 58, 93, 103, 157.
- Lane, J (2001). *A Social History of Medicine*. London: Routledge
- Rivett, G. (1). *The Development of the London Hospital System. The Voluntary Hospitals*. Article available: http://www.nhshistory.net Search 'Voluntary Hospitals' Last accessed 10/3/2017.
- Wiveliscombe Dispensary & Infirmary. 2 pamphlets held at Somerset Heritage Centre. Ref No A\AG1/1/20
- Wiveliscombe Infirmary Minutes, 1816-1835. Held at Somerset Heritage Centre. Ref No. DD\X\LXN/5/1/1
- Guy, J. *Malachi's Monument, The Taunton & Somerset Hospital*. 1986
- Jarman, S G (1890). *The Bridgwater Infirmary. A record of its rise and progress..* St. Ives, Hunts: Jarman & Gregory, "Guardian" Offices.
- Bridgwater Infirmary Records, *Management Committee (and friends of the Charity) minutes, 1813-1858*. Held at Somerset Heritage Centre. Ref No D\H\b/1/1
- Bridgwater Infirmary Reports, 1820-1848. Held at Somerset Heritage Centre. Ref No. D\H\b/2/1
- *Short History of Bridgwater Hospital*. Unknown author (n.d.). Held at Somerset Heritage Centre since 1986. Ref no D\H\yeo/23/2/2
- Woodward, J (1974). *To do the sick no harm – A study of the British voluntary hospital system to 1875*. Routledge & Kegan Paul

Chapter 8 – Ups and Downs

- Jarman, S G (1890). *The Bridgwater Infirmary. A record of its rise and progress..* St. Ives, Hunts: Jarman & Gregory, "Guardian" Offices.

- Bridgwater Infirmary Records, *Management Committee (and friends of the Charity) minutes, 1813-1858.* Held at Somerset Heritage Centre. Ref No D\H\b/1/1
- Squibbs, P J (1968). *A Bridgwater Diary 1800-1967.* Bridgwater: Squibbs.
- Toogood, J. *Public Institutions for the relief of the sick.* Prov Med Surg J 1841; s1-3: 59
- Toogood, J. *Dr Toogood on Medical Charitable Institutions.* Br Med J 1863; s1: 355

Chapter 9 – Professional Colleagues

- Sotis, W. *The 19th century British Post.* Available :
http://randombitsoffascination.com/2012/09/20/the-british-post/ Last accessed 11/3/2017
- *Collection of 11 letters to Jonathan Toogood,* 1810-1843. Held at King's College London Archives. GBO100TH/PP69 Toogood
- Munk, W. 2009. *Robert Willan.* Royal College of Physicians, Lives of Fellows. Available at http://rcplondon.ac.uk Last accessed 11/3/2017
- The Worshipful Society Of Apothecaries of London. *Our History.* Available at http://www.apothecaries.org/society/our-history
- Hunter, K. *Dr John Clarke: licentiate in midwifery of the Royal College of Physicians of London.* Clin Med JRCPL 2002;2: 153-6
- *Sir Astley Cooper, His Life, Character, and Writings.* Prov Med Surg J 1841; s1-1:353
- Burch, D (2009). *Astley Paston Cooper (1768-1841), anatomist, radical, and surgeon.* JLL Bulletin: Commentaries on the history of treatment evaluation. Available at http://www.jameslindlibrary.org/articles/astley-paston-cooper-1768-1841-anatomist-radical-and surgeon/ Last accessed 8/7/2016
- *Baron Guillaume Dupuytren.* Available at http://www.whonamedit.com/doctor.cfm/1104.html Last accessed 8/7/2016
- *Philibert Joseph Roux.* Available at http://en.wikipedia.org/wiki/Philibert_Joseph_Roux Last accessed 12/7/2016
- Pashkov.K A, Betekhtin M S. *Phillippe Ricord – prominent venereologist of the X1X century.* Isotoriâ mediciny. 2014. N4 (4). P. 13-17
- Ricord, P. *Course of lectures on Venereal Infections delivered at the Hôpital du Midi, Paris.* Prov Med Surg J 1843; s1-6: 323
- Toogood, J. *On the use of the speculum.* Prov Med Surg J 1841; s1-2: 86
The Late John Blackall, MD. BMJ 1860; s4-1: 75
- *Turner, Thomas.* Available at http://livesonline.rcseng.ac.uk/biogs/E003331b.htm Last accessed 8/7/2016

Chapter 10 – Toogood and the Law

- Lane, J. (2001). Medical Care under the Old and the New Poor Law. in: *A Social History of Medicine.* London: Routledge. p44-67.
- *Poor Law Amendment Act 1834.* Available at:
https://en.wikipedia.org/wiki/Poor_Law_Amendment_Act_1834 Last accessed 10/3/2017
- *The Bridgwater Workhouses.* Available at:
http://www.bridgwatertowncouncil.gov.uk/history/19th-century/the-bridgwater-workhouses/ Last accessed 10/3/2017
- *Bridgwater Union Workhouse.* Records held at Somerset Heritage Centre. Ref No A\BBC/10
- Toogood, J. *Parochial Medical Relief.* Prov Med Surg J 1843; s1-6: 276

- Woolrich, A P. *John Bowen 1785-1854.* Bridgwater Heritage Group. Available at: http://www.bridgwaterscientists.org.uk/bowen Last accessed 10/3/2017
- Sharp, D. *Thomas Wakley (1795-1862): a biographical sketch.* Lancet 2012; 379:1914-21
- Richardson, R. *Coroner Wakley: two remarkable eyewitness accounts.* Lancet 2001; 358:2150-54
- Toogood, J. *On inquests held before non-medical coroners.* Prov Med Surg J 1841; s1-1: 308
- Lane, J. *Observations on the conduct of coroners.* Prov Med Surg J 1844; s1-7: 358
- Trevor, W. *Case of Poisoning: Coroner's Inquest.* Prov Med Surg J 1845; s1-9: 445
- Toogood, J. *Observations on the mode of conducting coroner's inquests.* Prov Med Surg J 1845; s1-9: 476
- ANON (A. Surgeon). *Coroner's Inquests.* Prov Med Surg J 1845; s1-9: 534
- ANON (A Medical Coroner). *Coroner's Inquests.* Prov Med Surg J 1845; s1-9: 560
- Sopwith, H. *Coroner's Inquests.* Prov Med Surg J 1845; s1-9: 571
- Stead, H. *Coroner's Inquest: Abuse of the office of coroner.* Prov Med Surg J 1847; s1-11: 277
- Prichard, A. *Coroners' Inquests.* Prov Med Surg J 1848; s1-12: 502
- Ford, C. *Coroners and Medical Witnesses.* Prov Med Surg J 1849; s1-13: 641
- Toogood, J. *The present objectionable mode of conducting coroner's inquests.* Assoc Med J 1853; s3-1: 221
- Buchanan, C.A. *John Bowen and the Bridgwater Scandal,* Proc. SANHS 1987; 131: 181-201
- Bowen, J. New Poor Law. 1838. Held at Somerset Heritage Centre. Ref No DD\CLE/2/5
- Parliamentary Papers 1780-1849. *Minutes of evidence before the select committee on the Operation of the Poor law Amendment Act.* 25 June 1838, Vol. 19, Part 1: 725-752 & 9 July 1838, Vol. 19. Part 2.

Chapter 11 – The Great Arsenic Evil

- Whorton, J (2010). *The Arsenic Century.* Oxford: Oxford University Press.
- Stratmann, L (2016). *The Secret Poisoner.* New Haven: Yale University Press.
- Hemple, S (2013). *The Inheritor's Powder.* 2nd ed. London: Phoenix Press.
- Haslam, JC. Deathly décor: a short history of arsenic poisoning in the nineteenth century Res Medica 2013, 21 (1), pp.76-81 doi:10.2218/resmedica.v21i1.182
- Bartrip, P. *A "Pennurth of Arsenic for Rat Poison": The Arsenic Act, 1851 and the prevention of secret poisoning.* Medical History, 1992; 36: 53-69
- *Poisoning from Arsenic.* Prov Med Surg J 1841; s1-3: 257
- Tomkins, W. *Poisoning by Arsenic.-Coroner's Inquest.* Prov Med Surg J 1843; s1-6: 215
- Shearman, M. *On Arsenic as a Poison; Its tests and antidote.* Prov Med Surg J 1844; s1-8:3
- *Sarah Freeman – The Shapwick Murders.* Available at http://www.capitalpunishmentuk.org/freeman.html Last accessed 10/8/2016
- Toogood, J. (1845). Remarks of the Shapwick Poisonings. *The Lancet.* 45 (1131), 509.
- May, G P. *Case of poisoning by Arsenic; with remarks.* Prov Med Surg J 1845; s1-9: 453
- Toogood, J. *On the crime of secret poisoning.* Prov Med Surg J 1849; s1-13:362
South-Western Branch Meeting. Prov Med Surg J 1849; s1-13: 418
- PMSA 17th Anniversary Meeting. *Secret Poisoning.* Prov Med Surg J 1849: s1-13: 437

- Tunstall, J. *The Sale of Arsenic & the Prevention of Secret Poisoning.* Prov Med Surg J 1849; s1-13: 467
- Tunstall, J. *First Report of the Committee on the Sale of Poisons.* Prov Med Surg J 1850; s1-14:183
- PMSA 18th Anniversary Meeting. *Arsenic Committee.* Prov Med Surg J 1850; s1-14:460
- (1851). A Bill, Intitled "An Act to regulate the Sale of Arsenic. *The Lancet.* 57 (1442), 440-441.
- Tunstall, J. *Observations on the Sale of Arsenic Regulation Bill.* Prov Med Surg J 1851; s1-15: 181
- Cattell, T. (1852). On the "Sale of Arsenic Regulation Act". *The Lancet.* 59 (1481), 83.
- Annotations. (1929). The Sale of Arsenic. *The Lancet.* 214 (5537), 779-780.
- Jenson, W B. (2014) *The Marsh Test for Arsenic.* Available at http://www.che.uc.edu/Jensen/W.%20B.%20Jensen/Museum%20Notes/26.%20Marsh%20Apparatus.pdf Last accessed 12/3/2017
- Sale of Arsenic Regulation Act 1851. Available at www.legislation.gov.uk/ukpga/**1851**/13/en**act**ed Last Accessed 12/1/2017

Chapter 12 - Toogoodism

- Teal, A. *Quacks and Hacks: Georgian medicine and the power of advertising.* The Lancet 2014; 383 (9915), 404-405
- Clark, A J. *Universal Cures, Ancient and Modern.* Br Med J 1924; 2: 731
- *Quacks, Charlatans and Fakers – A History of Irregular Practice.* Available at https://quackscharlatansandfakers.wordpress.com Search James Graham Last accessed 12/3/2017
- Miller, W S. *Elisha Perkins and his Metallic Tractors.* Yale J Biol Med 1935. 8 (1): 41-57
- Grierson, J (1998). *Dr. Wilson and his Malvern Hydro.* Malvern: Aldine Press. 1.
- *Samuel Hahnemann.* Available at https://en.wikipedia.org/wiki/Samuel_Hahnemann Last accessed 21/9/2016
- Hastings, C. *Illustrations of the Water Cure, as practised at Malvern.* Prov Med Surg J 1842; s1-5:149
- Hastings, C. *Illustrations of the Water Cure.* Prov Med Surg J 1843; s1-5:328
- Mackness, J. *Itinerant Practice of the nineteenth century.* Prov Med Surg J 1843; s1-10: 435
- Fairplay, J. *On the Doctrines of Homeopathy.* Prov Med Surg J 1848; s1-12: 215 and 1848; s1-12: 330
- Cormack, J R. *On relations with Homeopathy.* Prov Med Surg J 1851; s1-15: 444
- PMSA 19th Anniversary Meeting. *Report on irregular practice.* Prov Med Surg J 1851; s1-15: 465-470
- Davies, W. *On the duty of the profession with reference to homeopathy and the other quackeries of the day.* Prov Med Surg J 1851; s1-15: 527
- ANON (FRCS). *Homeopathy.* Prov Med Surg J 1851; s1-15: 556
- *Homeopathy at Totness: Inquest.* Prov Med Surg J 1851; s1-15: 664
- PMSA 20th Anniversary Meeting. *Irregular Practice.* Prov Med Surg J 1852; s1-16: 399
- Toogood, J. *Prosecutions against Medical Men.* Br Med J 1863; 1: 386
- Fisher, P. Ernst, E. *Should doctors recommend homeopathy?* BMJ 2015; 351:h3735
- Toogood, J (1848). *Illustrations of the Fraud & Folly of Homeopathy.* London: John Churchill. pp. 3-26. [Electronic] Trinity College Library, Dublin [07 November 2013]

- Medical Toogoodism and Homeopathy. 1849 *British Journal of Homeopathy*. 7 (28), (April) pp.248-275. [Electronic] Trinity College Library, Dublin. [07 November 2013]

Chapter 13 – Family
- Ancestry.co.uk
- *1829 Boat Race – Where Thames Smooth Waters Glide.* Available at http://thames.me.uk/s00231a.htm   Last accessed 14/3/2017
- Diary of the Revd J J Toogood 1835-1850. Held at Somerset Heritage Centre. Ref No. DD/X/Bush
- Giles, J A. *Diary & Memoirs.* Held at Somerset Heritage Centre.
- Williamson, M. *Bundarra – Dr Charles Toogood.* Available at http://www.inverell.nsw.au/g-h-history-newsletter   Last accessed 14/3/2017

Chapter 14 – Legacy
- Bridgwater Infirmary Records, *Management Committee (and friends of the Charity) minutes, 1813-1858.* Held at Somerset Heritage Centre. Ref No D\H\b/1/1
- Jarman, S G (1890). *The Bridgwater Infirmary. A record of its rise and progress..* St. Ives, Hunts: Jarman & Gregory, "Guardian" Offices.
- Squibbs, P J (1968). *A Bridgwater Diary 1800-1967.* Bridgwater: Squibbs.
- *A Historical Tour of Ophthalmology.* Available at http://www.mrcophth.com Last accessed 13/3/2017
- Sorsby, A. *19th Century Provincial Eye Hospitals.* The British Journal of Ophthalmology. 1946. Available at http://bjo.bmj.com/content/30/9/501.full.pdf Last accessed 13/1/2017
- History of Moorfields Eye Hospital. Available at http://www.moorfields.nhs.uk/content/our-history

Appendix 1

GLOSSARY of just some of the 19TH CENTURY

REMEDIES used by TOOGOOD

- Antimony – metal, used in medicine since antiquity. Promotes sweating, vomiting and purging. Ingredient of Tartar Emetic. Still used today for some tropical diseases.
- Calomel – mercurous chloride, used as a purgative and treatment for Syphilis.
- Cod-liver oil – used for lung conditions particularly Tuberculosis
- Colocynth – 'Bitter Apple' 'Wild Gourd' – *Citrullus colocynthis,* found around the Mediterranean and Asia. Used as a purgative.
- Copaiba – resin from the trunk of several South American trees of the genus *Copaifera.* Used as a diuretic in dropsy.
- Dover's Powder – combination of Opium and Ipecac (ipecacuanha) developed by the physician Thomas Dover in 1732. Painkiller used up until the early 20th century, the emetic properties of ipecac preventing overdose.
- Fowler's Solution – arsenic solution (containing 1% potassium arsenite developed by Thomas Fowler in 1786). Prescribed as a tonic well into the 20th century.
- Griffith's Steel Mixture – used in Chlorosis
- Jalap – from Mexico, member of the bindweed family used as a powerful purgative.
- Mercury ointments – for syphilis
- Myrrh – resin from trees of the genus *Commiphori,* which grow in parts of the Middle East and the Horn of Africa. Used since ancient times for its astringent, antiseptic and aromatic properties. Especially used in Female Disorders.
- Peruvian Bark – *Cinchona* from South America contains Quinine, an anti-malarial, used to treat ague and other fevers
- Sammony – a gum resin from *Convolvulus scammonia* from the Eastern Mediterranean used as a purgative
- Squill – from the plant *Drimia maritime* native to southern Europe, western Asia and northern Africa. Used by the ancient Egyptians. Used as a diuretic in dropsy and as a laxative and expectorant.

Appendix 2

The Marsh Test

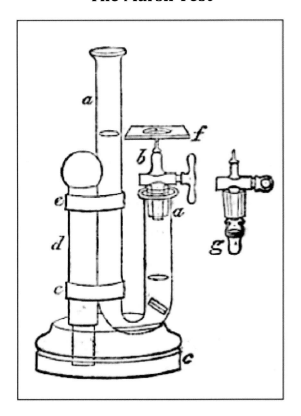

a – U-tube, b – stopcock (open), f – plate of glazed ceramic, g – stopcock (closed)

With the stopcock (*b*) in the open position, a piece of zinc (Zn) is placed in the shorter arm of the U-tube (*a*) and the tube filled with dilute sulphuric acid (H_2SO_4 (aq)) up to the stopcock. (Both reagents previously tested to ensure that they arsenic free)

The stopcock (*b*) is then closed and the sample to be tested for arsenic is added to the liquid.

If arsenic is present in the sample, the reaction that takes place generates a mixture of flammable gases – hydrogen gas (H_2) and arsine gas (AsH_3), which accumulate below the stopcock (*b*), forcing the liquid up the longer arm of the U-tube (*a*).

When enough gas has formed, the stopcock (*b*) is opened again and the gases are forced out the nozzle where they are then ignited, the flame touching a square plate of glazed ceramic (*f*)

If arsenic is present, a black mirror of elemental arsenic is deposited on the plate.

Notes on the Author

I trained as a doctor at The London Hospital (now The Royal London) in Whitechapel in the early 1970s and was surrounded by portraits of great medical men such as William Blizard and Frederick Treves. I went on to have a varied medical career, starting out as a General Practitioner and Police Surgeon in south-east London but after a move to Somerset with my husband and young family, I switched to Gynaecology and Contraceptive and Sexual Health. For a period of time I worked at both Bridgwater Hospital and Blake Hospital (the old Union workhouse).

I first became interested in medical history about six years ago and when I retired in 2012, I signed up for the History of Medicine Diploma course at the Worshipful Society of Apothecaries, held at the Apothecaries Hall in London. It was at this stage that I discovered the name Jonathan Toogood from Bridgwater in the British Medical Journal archives and wrote my diploma dissertation about this interesting 19th century surgeon. From then on I was hooked! I started to give talks to local WI and History Society groups and became convinced that there was a story to be told to the wider public. I have not attempted to write an academic book but I hope I will give the reader some insight into medical history and the life of a surgeon in the early 19th century. Despite the difficulties in the NHS, we would not be where we are today, with our modern medical services, without early pioneers such as Jonathan Toogood, who strove valiantly to improve the care of the sick.

Dr Lesley Sutcliffe 2017

Acknowledgments

I am grateful to the following people and organisations for their help with this book – the staff at the Somerset Heritage Centre who have been very helpful finding me documents and patiently reminding me how to use the microfiche; the staff at the Dorset History Centre in Dorchester and the Somerset and Dorset Family History Society in Sherborne; the staff at the Wellcome Library, the Kings College Archives and St Bartholomew's Hospital Archives in London; the staff at Torquay Library; Helen McGinley at the Department of Early Printed Books and Special Collections, Trinity College, Dublin for finding me copies of Medical Toogoodism and Homeopathy and Illustrations of the Fraud and Folly of Homeopathy and for sending them to me electronically. Thanks also go to Tony Woolrich at the Blake Museum, Bridgwater who gave me access to sketches and photographs held at the museum. The British Medical Journal Archives have also been a wonderful online resource. Other contributions for which I am grateful came from Jenny McCubbin for her photographs, David Bradshaw for his computer skills and my daughter Amy Dawson for checking my chemistry! Mention should also be made of The Worshipful Society of Apothecaries, whose Diploma course gave me the means and inspiration to pursue this project.

However, the most important person has been my husband David, who encouraged me to write this story and has given up so much of his time editing and preparing the book for print.

Index (Numbers in **bold** refer to illustrations)